The **9** *Rights of Every Writer*

The 9 Rights of Every Writer

A GUIDE FOR TEACHERS

Vicki Spandel

HEINEMANN
Portsmouth, NH

Heinemann
361 Hanover Street
Portsmouth, NH 03801–3912
www.heinemann.com

Offices and agents throughout the world

The author and publisher wish to thank those who have generously given permission to reprint borrowed material:

"How the World Makes Horses" by Jessie Haas. Copyright © 2005 by Jessie Haas. Used by permission of HarperCollins Publishers.

Library of Congress Cataloging-in-Publication Data
The 9 rights of every writer : a guide for teachers / Vicki Spandel.
    p. cm.
   Includes bibliographical references and index.
   ISBN 0-325-00736-5 (alk. paper)
    1. English language—Rhetoric—Study and teaching. 2. English language—Composition and exercises—Study and teaching. 3. Report writing—Study and teaching. I. Title: Nine rights of every writer. II. Spandel, Vicki.

PE1404.A13 2005
808'.042'0711—dc22   2005006656

Editor: Lois Bridges
Production: Lynne Costa
Cover design: Catherine Hawkes, Cat & Mouse
Interior design: Joni Doherty
Typesetter: Tom Allen, Pear Graphic Design
Manufacturing: Louise Richardson

Printed in the United States of America on acid-free paper
09   RRD   5

For Jack

because it is my deepest hope
that you will love to write &
that your voice will be heard.

Contents

Acknowledgments

At an IRA Conference a year or so ago, I had an engaging conversation with a woman sitting in the front row of my session on six-trait writing. She had been nodding vigorously throughout the session and later, as I was packing to make room for the next presenter, we began talking about writers—their needs and their rights. The right to be heard, to find a personal voice, to be assessed thoughtfully and compassionately, to make writing process not an external structure but a part of their thinking. *"This,"* she said, her eyes afire, *"this* is your next book! Don't you see? This *is the book!"*

And just like that, the book was born. Inspired by a conversation, an animated, knowing presence that would not be denied. The animated presence was Cindy Marten, Vice-Principal, Central Elementary, San Diego City Schools, and, I am proud to say, my good friend and mentor. She is a fireball, a thinker, and a driver. How lucky for me. Thank you, Cindy, for daring to think that our conversation could grow into a collection of essays, and for pushing me right off a cliff to make that happen. So often through this book, you have been what Mem Fox calls a "watcher"—a person whose face you see and whose words you hear as you write. A person who keeps you on track and listens for your voice. I so hope you love the book because its heart and soul belong to you.

I am also deeply indebted to the nine remarkable, talented writers whose own essays grace this book: Christine Kling, Tom Newkirk, Bob Ornstein, Sneed B. Collard, Bruce Ballenger, Jim Burke, Samantha Abeel, Steve Kramer, and Barry Lane. I believe any book is enriched through the sharing of multiple voices, and I am honored not only by the presence of these extraordinary writers, but by the eloquence of their expression and the insights that they so willingly offered. Each of them responded to my request for "writer's insights" with an eagerness that touched me deeply. A writer's life is always incredibly busy, and I thank you, each of you, for taking time to reach out to students and teachers in this way.

In addition, my heartfelt thanks to all the student writers who so generously allowed me to incorporate samples of their work. You are the reason for the book, after all. I am especially grateful to Nikki Henningsen, Jason Kelleher, Laura Schweigert, Rachel Woods, and to the students of Steve Kramer and Ellen Tatalias, two of the finest writing teachers around. Their students took time to reflect on the power of writing process and to offer their personal advice (Chapter 4) for making it work well.

No one has ever had a finer editor to work with than I had on this book. I could easily fill a tenth chapter with accolades for the support I received from Lois Bridges. Lois, it has been an honor and a joy to work with you. No one in history has ever answered emails faster or provided so many comforting answers. Bravo.

Thanks also to my wonderful family who allowed me once again to turn the whole house into a work station and who so patiently put up with the author's running joke: "I'll finish the book this week."

Preface

This is a book about creating *writing* that is a voice, not an echo. In this time when standards are all around us, and assessments to ensure that we and our students are meeting those standards are prevalent, it is useful to pause and reflect about why and how we teach writing—and whether it is a voice or an echo that we seek. So this is my heartfelt conversation with teachers—with you—about writing issues that matter to me: time for reflection, self-selection of topics, personalizing process, writing with our students, favoring individual path-finding over formula, and respecting the sacred individual voice that is the fabric of each student's cultural and personal identity.

Underlying each chapter is my philosophy about why we teach writing in the first place. Our reason is not—or at least it *should* not be—to help students meet the standards

Too often, young artists paint before they think. Over the years, I have disciplined myself to think before I paint. When I see a paintable subject or interesting situation, I paint more than I see. I paint what is to be seen. I paint what is inside me. I personalize the scene, make it my own so that through my painting, you and I, viewer and artist, can communicate. My goal is to create paintings that are a voice, not an echo.

—CHARLES WYSOCKI
Heartland

we set. Things like writing in multiple genres and for multiple purposes, developing and expressing ideas clearly and supporting them with evidence or detail, using language effectively and correctly, organizing information to promote understanding, or applying conventions correctly and in a way that enhances meaning and voice are all skills critical to good writing. All are worth teaching, and worth assessing. But they are a means to an end, not an end in themselves.

Writing, like painting, combines the best of observation with the artist's unique vision of the world. It encourages a deepened understanding of things that are hard to grasp. Writing encourages writers to think reflectively, to keep ideas in their heads for a long time. To change their minds. To tear their beloved construction down, right to the foundation, and build it anew. And because writing demands that we see everything from a clump of grass to the face of a child as if for the first time, writing makes teachers of us all.

Bruce Ballenger, a contributing author for this book, says that "Perhaps the best test of any writing is whether, after having read it, we see the world just a little bit differently" (2004, 295). *That* is a significant reason to teach writing: to encourage our children to create text that might change how others see things. Text that might, by extension, change the world. A hard thing to measure, of course, but definitely worthy.

In this book, I touch on what I believe to be the most worthwhile goals of writing: writing to think, to move another person, to create something that will be remembered, to find the most salient personal topics that will weave a common thread through virtually all the writing text in one's life, to develop a unique personal voice with which one feels at home, to develop and maintain a spirit of unrelenting curiosity that drives the writing forward, to be wholly comfortable with the act and process of writing. These are all hard things to measure. Moreover, they take time. Significant time. Heavy emphasis on assessment can rob us of that precious time. It can also make us afraid.

Fear is a poor place from which to write—or to teach. It kills the very things we need most to make our writing successful: genuine curiosity, tolerance of early efforts, trust in our own vision, willingness to risk, focus on personal questions, and passion for writing.

Fear can also drive us to take shortcuts in an effort to achieve writing success quickly. By shortcuts, I mean things like assessing students' work for them rather than teaching them to be assessors of their own and others' writing; explaining writing process instead of modeling it; assigning topics for our students so they will not need to search the world or their own hearts; or resorting to formulaic ways of organizing writing in the hope that a ready-made framework will make the task easier. I believe we pay a price for these shortcuts, and it is high. For little gains today, we trade away the best of tomorrow—our students' chances to discover what matters to them, and to write something others will want to read.

We stand at a crucial crossroad. We have been brought here by our efforts to make instruction and assessment work in harmony, to define through standards and personal goals what matters most in writing, and to assess it well in order to make instruction better. At its best, assessment can enormously enhance instruction by helping us identify both problems and strengths that might otherwise go undiscovered. At its best, instruction can give us insights not only about content but about ourselves. But assessment must focus on what matters, not on what's easy to measure. We must choose to make it do this. And instruction must go well beyond anything assessment can effectively measure to those deeper reasons for writing. We must choose to take it to that level.

The problem with standards is not that they aim too high but that often they do not lift us up nearly enough. The great irony is that when we teach writing for the right reasons—to help our children write with passion and touch the hearts of readers—the little things tend to fall into place anyway. We get the topic sentences and details and strong verbs we hoped to see because those little things help the writer reach her loftier goal. What's more, the writer learns to care about such things, not because we said she should, but because these writer's skills took her where she wanted to go all along, to a place where her writing became powerful.

Bruce Ballenger and I share an affinity for the writing of naturalist David Quammen. In *The Curious Researcher*, Ballenger says about Quammen's work: "Readers respond to an individual writing voice. When I read David Quammen . . . it rises up from the page, like a hologram, and suddenly, I can see him as a distinct individual. I also become interested in how he sees the things he's writing about" (2004, 232). There, in a nutshell, is the thing I would most wish for our student writers: that their personal voice would "rise up from the page, like a hologram" and keep me breathless to discover what they think. I cannot—and neither should you—settle for anything less.

I asked nine writers to join me in this conversation, to share for you—and, at your discretion, for your students—their writers' perspectives on how writing really works. So what you have is not necessarily a textbook version of writing, but more a collection of insiders' thoughts that give new dimension to the related topics I explore.

Novelist Christine Kling talks about her personal need for reflective time to clear her head and assemble thoughts. Author and teacher Tom Newkirk addresses a subject related to personal topic selection: the incorporation of violence in student writing. Bob Ornstein tracks his evolution as a writer, and tells of his search for a personal writing coach who would give him truly useful feedback. This thoughtful essay offers numerous insights on coaching well. Science writer Sneed B. Collard provides us with an up close look at his own personal writing process and the interesting ways it parallels or differs from what many students do in the classroom. Author and university teacher Bruce Ballenger tackles a controversial topic—the art of (and need for) writing badly in order to truly get at meaning. Jim Burke, author and high school teacher, addresses the need for all teachers to write. We cannot understand the challenges and decisions student writers face, Burke tells us, unless we do it ourselves. Award-winning author Samantha Abeel writes an open letter to assessors, asking them to look beyond the superficial to the underlying meaning—and to the writer.

Teachers, she insists, need to be trail guides for their students. In a thoughtful look at assessment and instruction, science writer Steve Kramer pits formulaic writing against a more individually driven approach, helping us sort out the outcomes and repercussions of each. Finally, in a comic and courageous "confession," writer and teacher Barry Lane explores the benefits—and sometimes unpredictable consequences—of trying on another voice.

Like writing, teaching is a brave thing to do. You are asked to give so much, with little but your own faith in yourself to assure you that what you are doing is right and will reap benefits. It is my hope this book will give you a small measure of courage to know how good your teacher instincts really are—and a few ideas that may inspire you to keep the conversation going.

One
The Right to Be Reflective

I was three when I first experienced the mystical place known as the Boundary Waters, a country of pristine wilderness, one of the few places on earth where wolves still claim their hunting territory without compromise. Chains of deep, startlingly clear lakes stretch from the arrowhead country of Minnesota so far to the north you cannot navigate them all within your lifetime. Granite outcroppings form natural diving platforms and picnic areas, but also sometimes sneak up from beneath the water to remind you that this is a wild place, not an amusement park, and you would do well to keep your wits about you.

We need wild places. They call to us. When we cannot get to them, we bring them into our world. In *Cultivating Delight*, natural history writer Diane Ackerman suggests that "people work hard to create a savannah-like environment in such improbable sites as formal gardens, cemeteries, and suburban shopping malls, hungering for open spaces" (2001, 83).

It is this hunger that pulls me back to the Boundary Waters again and again. From the moment I return, memories wash over me like waves. I see my father maneuvering a small fishing boat, years ago, easing up to the dock in his red flannel shirt and khaki hat, proudly displaying the catch of walleye he would fillet to perfection. "Watch for bones," he'd always say, as we tore into the fish too quickly. We did, but we never found even a small one. His deft hands had been too good with the knife. I see my barefoot grandmother, walking over the golden sand with the grace and elegance of a queen, bending to scoop up a wriggly salamander, handing it to me almost reverently,

I have come to believe that all essays walk in rivers. Essays ask the philosophical question that flows through time—How shall I live my life? The answers drift together through countless converging streams, where they move softly below the reflective surface of the natural world and mix in the deep and quiet places of the mind. This is where an essayist must walk, stirring up the mud.

—KATHLEEN DEAN MOORE
Riverwalking

and winking as my giddy, squeamish aunts cringed and squealed in the background.

Smells spark the strongest sensory memories. Even now, a hint of wood smoke calls up for me the aromatic scent of sauna fires drifting across the water at dusk, and the exhilaration of that telling moment when we ventured from the dry, penetrating heat of the sauna and plunged into the severe cold of the lake. This will surely kill us, we thought as we leapt from the dock, but surrendering ourselves to the embrace of the water, we felt more alive than ever. And later, listening to haunting, unmistakable call of loons across the water, we fell into a sleep so deep not even the midnight thunder could wake us.

Last summer, when my husband and I returned to this place that tugs at our hearts, our passion was kayaking. Picture a vast lake at dawn, still, heavy, glassy, the first coppery light spilling across the black water. Two loons are teaching their chick to dive, alternately slipping beneath the water, disappearing into the depths, and moving silent as shadows below the surface, while baby awaits their return. The little chick is bewildered at first, and somewhat frightened to see first mom, then dad, depart without even the briefest farewell. He is a tiny thing, a downy cork bobbing alone on miles of water, and beneath him swim northern pike fifty times his weight. He would rather, at first, adjust to his loss than risk following the parent loons under. Who can blame him? But loons are the most patient of teachers. They are undaunted by fear, by reluctance, by initial lack of skill. Again and again, they dive and resurface. They coax, they model, they never force. Little by little, baby gets the idea, ducking his bill, his head, then his whole neck—and finally going deep into the cold to swim with the fish. Eventually, he'll outswim most of them, but you have to look closely, with a teacher's eye, to see the predator of consummate skill and cunning that this tiny chick will become.

We are reluctant, always, to disturb the loons, who have raised instruction to so fine an art. So we slip our kayak as gently into the water as our strength will permit, easing down deep into our seats, our legs stretched out before us. You sit low in a kayak, and feel the cold of the lake wash around you. You become part of the water in a way a boat or canoe will not permit. A kayak is also one of the quietest water vessels—our run this morning is so silent we can hear our own breathing, hear the drips of water from our paddles hit the smooth face of the lake. The loons recognize us for the intruders that we are, but remain warily afloat. A half hour of rhythmic paddling takes us four miles to the well-named Elephant Rock, where the Dead River begins its dark and silent journey to an even more secluded lake. We stop to open a thermos of coffee that warms our wet hands. A blue heron fishing from a low dock is well aware of our arrival, but remains focused on the water, never looking up. He spears a silver fish on the first try, and flexing his great wings, takes off without a sound.

Adrift on the lake, floating at the whim of the waves—this is how freedom feels. This is how it feels to be *away*. Nothing rings, beeps, buzzes, flashes, or blinks. The mind takes in one image at a time and holds on, sometimes forever. The heartbeat slows. It is a place I visit often in my mind, and I am there even now. I feel the rock of the kayak as I write this. Later tonight, when our yoga instructor, Mariah, says to the class, "Take yourself to a place where you feel a sense of peace," this is where I will go. To Elephant Rock. To the cold of the water on my fingers and the smell of the wood smoke. To the call of the loon celebrating its chick's newfound courage. This is my refuge and my retreat, and it is a place all writers need.

What occurred to me as I sat there on that July morning, coffee warming my hands, no particular goals in mind, no deadlines to meet, was that a week in the Boundary Waters would be, for many students, more useful preparation for writing—or for writing assessment—than many of the frenzied drills and practice we feel we must provide. A mind freed is a powerful thing. A mind buffeted from all sides must spend most of its energy defending the fortress of inner tranquility that is essential to a writer's survival.

We are buffeted routinely these days—by traffic, flashing lights, horns and sirens, news talk radio, and cell phone users who insist upon sharing their personal lives with us. Television is a particularly intrusive culprit. Watching the news has become disarmingly stressful, due not only to the generally grim content, but also to the fact that information is now wielded like a weapon. While one anchorperson or another is firing primary headlines at us (set to the sort of music usually reserved for epic motion pictures), reinforcements wait in the wings with on-site updates that allow us to be mentally brutalized in real time. As these people speak, and as they barrage us with video, subtext parades across the screen in an incessantly interruptive ticker, requiring us to read one thing while listening to another and viewing yet another. Isn't this the very sort of multitasking we've warned our students to avoid in the classroom? Nor is that the end of it. In case our ability to focus is not yet sufficiently challenged, pop-up blurbs of weather, sports scores, and today's market gains and losses vie for our attention like bouncy children in the lower right corner, while a summary of what's coming next (just in case we're growing bored with the current onslaught) hurls flashing lights and somersaulting icons at us from lower left.

We worry whether our children can read with full engagement and understanding. We worry that they do not listen carefully or thoughtfully or for extended periods. We fear that they do not think about what they have read or learned or try to envision how it applies to their lives. Our answer? To design schizophrenic technology that says to them, "Don't worry. You can read and listen at the same time. You can think about different reports simultaneously. See? *Everyone* is doing it. It's easy! And besides, with all the information we have to share these days, you really cannot afford to spend too long on any one thing." If we had sought a way to minimize young viewers' attention spans as much as possible, we could hardly have come up with a more ingenious method. We have turned impatience and restless disengagement into normal states of mind. We have rendered contemplation all but dysfunctional.

We are said to live in the Information Age, but I wonder. Is that an accurate label for these times? Could the Information Superhighway be a gigantic one-way street? We are assaulted by information relentlessly. But how much are we absorbing? Many current movies and television programs are filmed in a jarring, jumping style that's considered stylish. It's the twenty-first century, for God's sake. We don't have time to focus. It's all happening at once, and we mustn't miss a beat. We move compulsively from one sight, one scene, one experience to another. There is always a more thrilling, more stirring moment coming. If one film features five explosions, two leaps from burning buildings, and four car chases, another must double this count to remain competitive. Dialogue? Scenery? How dull, how banal can you get? Unless, of course, they're filmed with special effects. Mountains as backdrop might seem boring, but mountains erupting or spawning avalanches could be dramatically acceptable. Two people talking: deadly dull. But two characters provoking each other into a bloodletting duel to the death—now that could work. We crave action. We seek volume in which to drown ourselves. Lyrics are screamed, not sung. Words and melody are secondary; percussion is the thing. We don't want our senses titillated; we want them bludgeoned.

As much as we revere noise, we fear silence. In the quiet, we are left with ourselves. And in our culture, there is deep fear of being alone. We must remain connected, or as one of my neighbors puts it, "I like to feel dialed-up."

One of the most endearing features of the Boundary Waters is that most cell phones cease to work there. In the charming and quaint cabin (built in 1940) where we stayed, the floors angled so much it took me four days to learn to stand on one leg long enough to put my jeans on in the morning. We literally walked uphill to the bathroom sink, and stepped downhill to open the oven. We loved it. There were no computer hookups, no DSL, no Internet—and so, no email. If you have seen a film in which an astronaut briefly detaches himself or herself from a spacecraft, you know how it feels to visit the North Woods. You are detached for a time, free-floating. Yes, things are (probably) going on back home. But for a brief and luxurious moment, you are not part of them. You take back control of your mind. Freed from the tyranny of electronic toys, you learn all over, like a small child left to his or her own devices, to entertain yourself.

In his masterful book *Testing Is Not Teaching*, Donald Graves talks extensively about long thinkers (2002, 53), those people with ability to sustain cogent thought over long periods, eventually developing a body of understanding or even a philosophy of life. I like to think these might be people who entertained themselves as children, who could look for a long while at a loon fishing, people who drink in silence and have no fear of being alone. Long thinkers include people like Thomas Jefferson, Albert Einstein, Toni Morrison, or Charles Darwin, people who sustain focus, go deep inside a subject, and expand others' understanding of *big* topics—such as human rights, evolution, or ways of experiencing time. Topics that cannot be defined through multiple-choice tests, cannot be covered within the scope of a school curriculum, and cannot be mastered—ever.

Serious writing requires long thinking. I'm not talking about the writing required to complete a form or dash off a note on a get-well card or summarize a major goal in marketing. That sort of writing takes some skill in swimming on the surface, rather like the baby loon who has not learned to dive yet. Real writing, though, the sort we hope our students will aim for (say, a persuasive essay on global warming, a story of a teenager overcoming bigotry, a poem about learning to love someone society perceives as being "different," or research that answers the question of whether predatory animals will still walk the earth a hundred years from now), takes long thinking. It takes reflection, the courage to dive below the surface, the willingness to live with a topic for a long period of time, turn it over and over in your mind, and decide for yourself what questions to ask about it.

How do we open this door to reflective thinking for our students? We cannot, of course, take them on a voyageur trek to the wilderness. That is too bad, I think, because who knows what sort of writing might result if we said to our students, "Welcome to a different world of writing. A different kind of class altogether. I am not going to lecture or even coach you. I'm not going to assign *anything*. Instead, I'll simply take you away for a time, to a place where the mind lets go. We're just going to be alone with our thoughts—no radio, no television, no phones, no video games. We're going to kayak at dawn and watch the heron fish. We're going to sit on granite lookouts, curl our toes against the moss, and contemplate the ways a rainstorm colors the surface of a lake. At night, after we've warmed ourselves in the sauna and braved the cold of the lake, when the only light is from the stars, we will hold our breath and listen for the wolves to sing. Then, when we come home, we'll write." No, we cannot do that. We have to try to educate ourselves about writing at the most unlikely of all places—our desks. But as Diane Ackerman tells us, when you can't venture to the wilderness, you bring the wilderness to you. And because the mind has a powerful and natural capacity for reflection, there are many ways to do this: "The brain's genius is its gift for reflection. What an odd, ruminating, noisy, self-interrupting conversation we conduct with ourselves from birth to death. That monologue often seems like a barrier between us and our neighbors or loved ones, but actually it unites us at a fundamental level, as nothing else can" (Ackerman 2004, 4).

Commitment to reflection means having more respect for that internal monologue, whether we call it thinking, meditating, contemplating, or day-dreaming. It means abandoning our compulsion to feel dialed-up all the time. Giving ourselves opportunities to meander through the landscape of our own thought. For it is there in the quiet of our own minds, not on the evening news and not on the computer, that we learn to make sense of it all. It is there, in that internal world of the mind, that we develop the philosophy from which we write. If we want to encourage deep thinking, we must allow students to disconnect from the world occasionally, to venture outside the spaceship.

How do we foster such reflective thinking? First, we need to provide some quiet time—even if it is short-lived—for writers to think and write. Though this is admittedly a difficult thing to achieve in most school environments, we must respect many writers' need for silence by asking for it openly and by expressing and modeling our own need for quiet time to write. If we honestly use the time for writing, not for doing other things (planning lessons, conferring), we make quiet, reflective time something to value, even if it is elusive and hard to attain. When students see us write during this time, and when they hear us asking for silence in order to think clearly, we are teaching them that quiet time is something writers need.

Second, we can read aloud, often and for as long as possible. The capacity for reflective thinking often begins with hearing someone read to you—or even reading to yourself for the sheer joy of it. "Books saved my life," author Gary Paulsen tells us in his introduction to *Shelf Life* (2003, 1). He describes himself at thirteen, a virtual nonreader, taking a book the librarian had given him "to a hideaway I'd created behind the furnace where someone had abandoned a creaky old armchair under a bare lightbulb" (3). There, he struggled painfully through the text, taking over a month to read the first book, but never giving up because books transported him, literally, to another world, to a place he needed so badly to go, away from the pain of his arguing parents and into "a life outside myself that made me look forward instead of backward" (4).

The truth is, books save most of us. They take us on a journey of the mind. This is one reason we love them so much. They pull us away. They develop our imaginations, our ability to think, as Paulsen says, outside ourselves. They teach us to form whole landscapes out of tiny details, to envision characters so vivid they make us cringe or melt with compassion or fall in love, to recall our own history with breathtaking accuracy, to anticipate and predict, and to see things in ourselves we might otherwise have left uncovered. Best of all, every trip is different.

On one read-aloud journey, we might go with Dylan Thomas across the ocean, and peek in on *A Child's Christmas in Wales*:

One year was so much like another, in those years around the sea-town corner now and out of all sound except the distant speaking of the voices I sometimes hear a moment before sleep, that I can never remember whether it snowed for six days and six nights when I was twelve or whether it snowed for twelve days and twelve nights when I was six. (1978/1993)

Another time, we'll travel with Laura Hillenbrand back in time to the historic thoroughbred match race in which upstart Seabiscuit dares to rival the legendary War Admiral. We'll crowd right up to the rail and watch jockey George Woolf, riding Seabiscuit, battle it out with Charley Kurtsinger, on War Admiral:

> Woolf dropped low over the saddle and called into Seabiscuit's ear, asking him for everything he had. Seabiscuit gave it to him. War Admiral tried to answer, clinging to Seabiscuit for a few strides, but it was no use. He slid from Seabiscuit's side as if gravity were pulling him backward. Seabiscuit's ears flipped up. Woolf made a small motion with his hand.
> "So long, Charley." He had coined a phrase that jockeys would use for decades. (2001, 273)

Few of us will brave the Alaskan wilderness to run the Iditarod. But we might feel brave enough to hop on a sled with Gary Paulsen. As the writer this time, Paulsen knows he must make the whole reading journey as real for us as it was for him in those long-ago days, hiding out behind the furnace. He must take us into the world of the book, to a place so far from anything called home that being lost could mean never being found again:

> Cold came at me from everywhere. Any seam, any crack, any opening and I could feel jets of it, needles of it, deadly cutting edges of ice, worse than ice, absolute cold coming in.
> It was, simply, not believable. . . .
> I do not know how cold it became that night, not in degrees, not in the clinical, petty measurements that humans have come to use.
> I know it was so cold the wooden matches struck on the abrasive side of the box would not light no matter how fast or hard they were struck.
> I know it was so cold the batteries on my headlamp stopped functioning and I ran through the night in the dark—and the batteries were inside my clothing. . . .

Cold. So cold that when the sun came up and I felt the warmth on
my clothing . . . I was as grateful as I was when I got out of the army
or saw my son born—soul grateful. (1994, 228–230)

Thomas, Hillenbrand, and Paulsen are such skilled writers that when they invite
us to tag along, we accept in a heartbeat. But the magic of being read to tran-
scends the quality of the book itself. There is something inherently soothing
about using human words, interpreted by a human voice, to build within our
minds and hearts an internal world unique to each person's imagination. So we
can love the act of being read to even without loving the book.

I learned just how true this was when one day at Paulina Springs (the very
charming, well-stocked bookstore in the little town of Sisters, where I live), I
stumbled on the very book my fourth-grade teacher had read aloud to our class
so very long ago. I couldn't get over my luck. What a treasure, I thought. I
opened it in a rush. I could hardly wait to relive those lines I had inhaled after
every recess, remembering that sense of anticipation as we fell into our hard
wooden desks, still catching our breath, the perspiration drying on our necks as
the familiar words "Now then, where were we?" scooped us up and lowered us
gently back into the plot. As I read, though, my excitement receded like the
tide. Amazingly, the book held none of the color I'd remembered. The imagery
was flat, the dialogue wooden and forced, the plot exceedingly dull and slow
moving. What had happened? I realized with a start that what had made those
moments wondrous was not the book itself, but the deep and immeasurable
pleasure of being read to—the chance to escape, envision, pretend. To mentally stretch out.

A colleague said to me the other day, "Soon, you know, we won't have
books at all. Not the kind you put on shelves. Why would we? They'll all be on
the Internet—so much handier, and you can skip right to the part you like
best." I cannot imagine a world in which this would be true.

While technology may provide convenience, it offers little of the sensory
joy that is the whole purpose of going on a retreat. Why on earth would we sit
at attention, staring at a glary screen when we could curl our legs under a cozy
blanket, and pause in our reading to glance up at the fire or look out the window at the snowfall? How could we do without the feel of the books in our
hands, the weight and texture, the satisfaction of turning the pages, the joy of
going back to the cover to wonder over and over how the picture or the title connects to the text? How could we do without the smell of books, a smell that now
mingles with freshly ground coffee in many bookstores and (even if you are not
a coffee drinker) brings an instant sensation of peace and anticipation. How
could we do without the question, "Let's see now—where was I?" Then looking at the top of the book to discover, from the placement of the bookmark,

how much joy of discovery remains. How could we do without that moment when we put a book down and let the memory of a special word or phrase or whole passage sink into us and become part of us forever? How could we resist the temptation to have a conversation with the writer by making those little marginal notes that will remind us, five years from now, just what we loved so much? And when we long for someone to read to us, will we gather 'round the computer screen? No—when it comes to encouraging reflection, real books are just the ticket.

What else can we do to help our students become reflective thinkers? We can slow down the pace of classroom dialogue, and by our listening, encourage our students to speak more and to speak to each other. To have a true conversation, rather than filling in blanks as if they were on *Jeopardy*. We can remind ourselves how often there is more than one answer to a question, and teach ourselves to wait while students reason and collect their thoughts. My colleague Rick Stiggins, an assessment specialist, has visited countless classrooms to observe the strategies teachers use to coach their students to think. Part of this research led him to measure the length of time teachers tend to wait for a response after posing a question. In many cases, he tells us, it is not more than two to three seconds. Surely not enough for much deep thinking.

The first time I heard Rick talk about our compulsive need to fill the silence, it made me recall a high school teacher who asked us one day to define what a *symbol* was. Think for a moment how *you* would answer this question. *Time's up.* That is precisely how long—just the time it took for you to read those words—we were given. The first student called upon (no one ever volunteered in this class) ventured this definition: "A symbol is a representation of something else." The thundering "No!" that followed set us on edge, for most of us had an answer much like that one formulating in our minds, and now that it was not an option, we felt that first jolt of fear that stops learning in its tracks.

A second student was called upon almost instantly, and offered this: "A symbol is something that stands for something else." He didn't even finish before the word "Wrong!" was echoing through the classroom, bouncing off the walls, ringing in our heads. A third timid victim gave an explanation I liked: "A symbol is something that makes you think of something bigger, something beyond the object itself." At that moment, such abject derision filled the teacher's face that I expected acid to drip down his cheeks. He didn't even answer, just pivoted, eyes closed, until his finger pointed straight at me, like a rapier, poised. I froze. "It's just . . . just . . . ."

"Just *what*?!" he snapped. But I was choking. It was the ultimate humiliation. I couldn't even ratchet out a wrong answer, much less the correct one. We never did learn what a symbol was, in this man's mind. The lesson was not wasted, though. I have remembered it always, as a strategy for quelling reflective thinking, brilliantly modeled. Later, I looked up *symbolism* in the dictionary, and felt both validated and puzzled to find words very close to those my peers had expressed—along with this intriguing idea, that a symbol could be a thing visible representing or causing us to think of something invisible. Much the way the image of a solitary loon takes the mind across the water to a meaning that waits on the far shore.

If we wish to encourage reflective thought, we must stop equating thinking with busy-ness. I recall once hearing a teacher say, "I can tell the very first day of writing workshop who the real writers are. They plunge right in. They don't sit staring at the ceiling or looking out the window." As she was speaking, I grew increasingly nervous. "Uh-oh," I thought. "*I* stare at the ceiling. I take a *long* while to get going or to make any marks on the paper at all. She's talking about *me*."

Her words made me look at student writers in a new way, to begin noticing their habits of starting. Some eager writers *do* plunge right in—but so do many reluctant and one-line writers eager to get the whole thing over with. On the other hand, there are, it seems, many writers who, like me, are notorious starers and thinkers. Where did we get the idea that writing only occurs when a pencil is moving or a keyboard is clicking? So much of what is most productive in *any* work we do is silent and hard to observe. While a few students gazing out the window may be wishing themselves a thousand miles away, others could be pulling in the very thoughts that will be the foundation for their writing. Professional writers engage in this sort of behavior all the time, but when *they* do it, we are more tolerant. Diane Ackerman describes her efforts to give the study where she does much of her writing a "garden feel" with yellow walls, floral fabrics, and numerous plants. Her favorite spot for thinking and pulling together her ideas, Ackerman says, is right in front of the bay window: "I've had fun making sure certain flowers are ideally visible from that perch. I sometimes recline there in yellow and purple pillows, for hours, drinking tea and watching the birds and flowers. It's my favorite place to meditate, read garden books, or nap" (2001, 46). Should we tell her to quit staring out the window and get busy?

In an essay called "Through the Eyes of a Child," folk artist Charles Wysocki recounts the joy and necessity of an artist's going deep inside the mind to where the "pictures" are:

> I would spend hours staring out of the window. In school, the teacher would tap her pencil on the desk. Tap. Tap. Tap. "Wysocki, the classroom is in here." At home, my mother would ask me what I was looking at. "Pictures," I said.
>
> Even then, I was seeing more than was out there to see. I was

"making things up." These days it's called creative imaging. In that time and place, it was called daydreaming. (1994, 16)

"Making things up" is a critical part of painting or writing. Prewriting or rehearsing, writers call it. Assembling ideas, putting the pieces together, imaging and imagining. It fills the well. A writer who comes to the desk ready to write, to make the pencil move, has been writing already in his or her mind, turning ideas over and finding a place to begin the way an experienced fly fisherman eyes the river and finds the perfect spot to land that first cast. No one doubts that the fisherman is fishing long before the fly hits the water.

Time, not geography, is the key to good reflection. Not all writers have a river to stroll alongside or wilderness to walk through. But student writers may create an internal retreat by listening to music, looking at a painting, watching tropical fish, reading, drawing, or doing yoga. Any activity that allows the mind to create its own world will do.

Reflection is not just for students—or for writers. It is for everyone. Most especially, it is essential to the mental and emotional health of teachers. This is a time of continual professional development. Meetings and workshops promise us better ways of spending our time, organizing our classrooms, teaching reading and writing, integrating writing with all curricular areas, applying standards, preparing our students for tests, and nudging them toward higher goals, like attending college. Much of what we learn through formal professional development is invaluable. But while we are rushing about, missing one meeting for another, or making notes no one will ever read again, let's not underestimate the power of reflection. We need to find a quiet corner now and then where we can be alone to write a few therapeutic lines in a journal, compose a poem for a friend's birthday, or lose ourselves in a great book. These reflective activities are also professional development—of the highest order—even if they are not listed in catalogs or acknowledged with grades and certificates.

The late Charles Kuralt, a frequent visitor to the Boundary Waters, was overwhelmed by its sheer expanse, and summed it up this way:

A birch tree grows on the shore of Moose Lake. A canoe lies on the bank beside it.

From that birch tree, you could paddle the canoe up to the end of Moose Lake and camp overnight and put the canoe in another lake the next morning. You could cross that lake, and camp for the night, and paddle across another lake on the third day. You could keep this up, visiting a different lake every day, for a hundred years, and you still wouldn't get to all the lakes. (1995, 141)

Such is the power of reflective thought, that we can visit a different place within the mind every day and still have places deep inside ourselves to explore. Our personal wilderness is boundless. If we allow ourselves the joy, the luxury, of reflection, it will be hard to resist teaching it to our students. We will want them to appreciate what powerful thinkers they are, to go inside their own heads and listen to the echoes of their thoughts rolling long and far across the water.

FROM A WRITER'S NOTEBOOK

Reflection: The Path to Meaning

CHRISTINE KLING

I once had a nightmare about numbers on a chalkboard. Written in big block numerals was the time 11:15, the time when my test would be over. My watch read 11:11 and I was staring at a blank page. I awoke covered in sweat and terrified that I would never get into college.

The deadlines that I face today as a professional novelist are not all that different from that time written in yellow chalk on the board. Many times, my best work just does not flow on command. In school, I often couldn't get the words out before the proctor announced, "Pencils down," and today, I struggle mightily with deadlines until my New York editor finally emails me saying, "Just send me what you've got."

The famous American playwright Edward Albee once said, "I write to find out what I'm thinking about." Good writing requires a certain amount of reflection because writing is essentially making new connections in your brain. It is discovery, connecting the dots to form shapes and animals you didn't know were there. And in making these connections, it is important for a writer to take risks, to make connections that may seem all wrong, but to try them out in order to discover something new. Thus a good first draft, to my mind, is really a poor first draft because it means I didn't take risks.

Sometimes, though, this desire to write something better than just "good" can result in the paralysis we know as writer's block. It's as though there is a continuum, where at one end you find the lazy writer who doesn't care about discovering anything new—he just wants to get the work done, and will take the path of least resistance, regurgitating what he already knows. This writer is never blocked because he never bothers to reflect. At the other end of the continuum is the writer who is so determined to "make it new," she cannot finish anything. It is never good enough. The real world of deadlines means most professional writers must live somewhere in the middle of that continuum.

Once I manage to get over it, and realize it's OK to send my editor a less than perfect first draft of a novel, I am freed to write and let my imagination take me where it will. Sure, sometimes I still get stuck. Once, I wanted to find a new way to describe sea clouds at dawn. I was looking for a metaphor, and for almost three days I paced, I walked my dogs, and I tried to think of what it was those clouds looked like. Finally, I found these simple words and I wrote, "To the east, the sky had turned a whitish blue and the clouds low on the horizon looked like ash-covered charcoal with the glow of an occasional ember shining through."

I have discovered that the real joy of writing now comes during the editing process, from the way my editor makes me discover new connections by simply asking me questions:

- In Chapter 27, have you thought about getting B. J. to help Seychelle?
- Can you go a little further into the reasons why Malheur is so evil?
- What about developing Racine into a more central character?

Sometimes it takes a lot of stamina to respond to each question by thinking deeply about why I originally made certain choices and whether or not they were good choices. I take some risks that don't pan out, and that's OK because others work beautifully. Then, when I decide I need to change a passage, I ask myself, *How can I improve the text?* It is in reflecting on my writing through editorial input that I can finally produce work I like.

Writing teachers today face a peculiar paradox because we want our students to learn to reflect and revise in order to write something meaningful, yet our standardized tests assess these students via timed writings that leave little or no time for reflection or revision. What kind of message does that send these kids? No wonder they think of writing simply as a way to demonstrate what they know. It is up to teachers, then, to help them see that writing can show them what they *don't know*. As Rachel Carson said, "The discipline of the writer is to learn to be still and listen to what his subject has to tell him."

CHRISTINE KLING's *first novel,* Surface Tension, *featuring tugboat captain Seychelle Sullivan, was published by Ballantine Books in November 2002. The second in the series,* Cross Current, *came out in 2004. Christine completed her MFA in creative writing at Florida International University, and she works as a coordinator for the Magnet Programs of Broward County Public Schools in Fort Lauderdale.*

Two

The Right to Choose a Personally Important Topic

When I was in tenth grade, all we could talk about was "next year." That's because "next year," we would have the teacher from hell, the one everyone feared, the one who used sarcasm as a weapon (*Really? However did you come up with that answer, Mr. McKenzie? Enlighten us. . . .*), the one whose spelling lists contained words so esoteric (*toastieweirdoastie, eisteddfod, scire facias*) that few of us could pronounce them much less think how we might use them, the one with writing assignments so remote from routine human thought we couldn't imagine how to respond. His favorite: *Write 500 words about the inside of a pencil.* This assignment, given annually, earned him the nickname "Mr. Graphite."

> If we want students to write with voice, they must have real choice in their writing regarding content, organization, and form. As teachers of writing, it is our job to show students how to make responsible and gratifying decisions, as well as to negotiate possibilities with them.
>
> —REGIE ROUTMAN
> *Conversations*

It wasn't so much that we had no time to think about the assignment. This is often a problem on state assessments, where students are not allowed to see the prompts in advance, as if somehow this would be a form of cheating. There really is no way to cheat in writing—unless, of course, you have someone else do the writing for you—and advance warning is only of help in cases where it is useful to think about the topic. We had a whole year to think about the pencil. Since no one has been inside a pencil, however, there is no way to reflect on the experience or gather information or interview someone who has been there. You know only what your imagination feeds you.

My imagination transformed me into a termite who had burrowed into a tree and somehow escaped injury when the tree was milled and its wood processed into pencils. My piece began, "It's dark in here. I don't care. I like the dark." That is all I remember of what I wrote. Most of the students in my class wrote nothing. They had no insights about life inside a pencil. Mr. Graphite was quite heartless about all this. In his view, his assignment had nothing to do with their responses; they were simply irascible teenagers refusing to join in the joie d'vivre of his classroom and they deserved the failing grades they got.

As for me, I got a B+, that most frustrating of grades. The grade that says, "Ah—look at *that*. *So* close. What a shame." A B+ is like striking out after hitting ten foul balls. From Mr. Graphite's perspective, of course, this grade was a benevolent gift from heaven. He didn't give As. "*So* close" was as high as you could hope to go in his class.

Most of the writing we did for the rest of the year involved literary analysis. And we quickly figured out a few basics that reflected Mr. Graphite's way of viewing literature (and life): an essentially dark view of the universe may be construed as "realism"; in any book worth reading, the characters are either perpetrators or victims of the same malevolent forces that could strike any of us at any moment if we're not careful; happy endings are inferior, so the mature student will get over wishing for them.

Although we weren't having a very good time, and certainly weren't learning to think for ourselves, we were getting better at echoing the teacher's philosophy. So things were humming along. Then, something happened to Mr. Graphite about halfway through the year. He fell in love. Love mellowed Mr. Graphite to the point of oblivious nonchalance, and he did something quite startling and out of character: He got too busy (and probably too distracted) to think up any more outlandish assignments, and allowed us instead to choose our own topics. We exploded like confetti from a canister.

My best friend, Diedre, wrote about her tyrannical father, who terrorized his children into obedience. Her stories were frightening (yet fascinating) to read: stocking-cushioned footsteps thumping softly on the floorboards as Diedre's tall, blond father-turned-inquisitor came creeping down the hallways of their Victorian home. I could scarcely believe that this kindly looking gentleman I had met at Latin Club, the one with the soft, fat fingers, actually became Mr. Hyde after hours. The writing gave Diedre a therapeutic release tantamount to taking tranquilizers. Exhausted from drafting, she would invite me to proofread as she lay on the floor staring at the ceiling, her face absolutely expressionless. I threaded my way through her words as if navigating a verbal minefield. There wasn't a book we read for class as intriguing—or dark—as what Diedre wrote for class.

Our mutual friend Sam, who hadn't written anything all year, wrote first poetry, then song lyrics, and actually shared some of his songs in class— imagine Bob Dylan off-key (*more* off-key). He wrote about love and war and marrying someone your parents disapproved of—something none of us had done yet, but a seemingly romantic notion we thoroughly enjoyed pondering.

He did not play the guitar well, but he did play with enthusiasm, and since most of us felt shy even reading our writing aloud, singing your words seemed a bold step. We thought him very brave, and vigorously applauded every performance. Mr. Graphite awarded him a standing ovation one day, and Sam's GPA soared.

I wrote about my horse. She was boarded on a remote farm in North Dakota, and I had to ride the train for twelve hours to be with her. (It wasn't a place to which you could fly.) We spent long days, dawn to dusk, roaming the prairies of western North Dakota, no one knowing where we were. It was, for me, a time of escape. I loved the freedom and loved the horse who took me there. One day as I was riding the perimeter of the wheat fields, a man in an old blue pickup pulled alongside me to ask if he could buy my horse. He offered me $100—a respectable if not impressive price at the time. I laughed and said she was not for sale, and later wrote about how some things had no price tag. The story was called "A Hundred Dollars." The notion that some bits of life are priceless was hardly original, but it was my first wholly passionate piece of writing, the first thing I remember writing completely for myself, without caring whether anyone else, including the teacher, might like it. For me, this was a breakthrough moment; not because the writing was so fine but because, like Sam and Diedre, I had discovered the matchless satisfaction of writing about something that mattered to me.

You'll often hear it said that the kind of restrictive topic development we knew in the early months of Mr. Graphite's class exists only in the world of school; that out there, in the real world, writers choose their own topics. That's often true, but not always. Technical and corporate writers are called upon to create textbooks, manuals, brochures, advertising and public relations pieces, guidelines and directions for a wide range of specific subjects, and usually have minimal creative control over content. For some writers, that's a very comfortable place to be. Thinking up a new topic is freeing, but it's also a lot of work.

As a staff writer for *Willamette Week* paper, I usually began a new article by presenting my editor, Alice, with an idea for my column—say, the effects of stress on health. She would either approve it or ask for another suggestion. But the original concepts were all mine. No one threw me suggestions, and sometimes, I used to wish they would. There's a certain pressure in coming up with something both newsworthy and interesting. Yet this is what skilled writers must do.

Charles Kuralt retired from his job with CBS News in 1994, but he did not retire from writing at that point. How lucky for us. He planned one last trip, a glorious expedition to his favorite sites throughout the United States, then wrote of them in a collection called *Charles Kuralt's America*. Though I don't know this for a fact, I seriously doubt that the editor said to Charles Kuralt one day, "Charles—why don't you take a trip and then you could write about your travels? Your topic for the first chapter will be to describe for the reader what it is like to live in New York City. Make your description so clear that a reader can feel just how it is to be in New York." More likely, Kuralt came up with the concept for the book. He chose the sites that would best reflect his vision of America, and chose these words to introduce the final chapter—"December: New York City":

> Nobody lives in New York City . . . We live in our neighborhoods. These are small towns just like those in Iowa or Nebraska, except that they are not surrounded by farm fields; they are surrounded by other small towns. We have our own small-town drugstores and barbershops and hardware stores and cafés, and we know the mail-man by his first name, and we say hello to our neighbors on the street, including the dogs and cats. (1995, 261)

Kuralt goes on to describe one of his neighbors, Alice, a woman who nostalgically recalls the smell of Montana sage, but who moved, alone, to New York at age twenty-seven because she could not resist the chance to hear Wagner for one dollar at the old Met. A less experienced writer might have gone methodically on to expand his description of the drugstore or barbershop. A true writer knows to tell me about Alice and the old Met. Kuralt proceeds to describe his favorite neighborhood restaurant, the Beatrice, where he "can drop in at the spur of the moment" because "the first definition of a neighborhood restaurant is that you don't have to make a reservation" (263). I can smell the veal and the pasta, hear the soft hum of music and conversation, and see the golden glow from sconces decked with holly cuttings. I feel I am right there, in a corner booth, and I am so grateful to Kuralt for coming up with these very images, these precise details—because who else would have thought of them? I wouldn't, certainly. I doubt his editor would have either. With unassigned, original, and personal writing come surprises.

Similarly, I doubt anyone said to Margery Facklam, "Write a book about an animal or creature you find fascinating. For example, you might choose to write about the spider." I do not know Margery, but I know she has two things any writer needs: curiosity and a talent for choosing the right detail. This is not unlike the talent some people have for selecting a good gift. Same principle, really. You think about the person you're choosing the gift for, but in the end, you choose something you'd like to receive yourself. So here we are unwrapping the gift Margery has chosen for us, a description of the golden silk spider:

> The web of the golden silk spider, Nephila, is so strong that it can trap a bird in flight or entangle a person running through the woods. In woodland clearings of the Gulf Coast of Alabama and northern

Florida, Nephila spiders the size of saucers often spin orb webs as wide as garage doors.
. . .
The people of the South Sea islands, in the Pacific Ocean, know how to trick Nephila into making fishing nets for them. They bend long bamboo poles in a loop at one end and stick the other end in the ground. During the night the spiders weave their thick webs on these handy frames. In the morning, the islanders pull the bamboo sticks out of the ground and go fishing with their spider-made nets. (2001, 8)

I love this description, and I want to say to Margery Facklam the same thing I say when I get any great gift: "It's just what I wanted! How did you think of it?" My Aunt Elva used to pick out her own gifts, wrap them herself, and even write the gift tag so it would say what she wanted to hear: "To Elva with a world of love from Gus." Assigning writing is like picking out and wrapping our own gifts. We get what we *think* we want, but we also give up the chance for a wonderful surprise from someone who might know us better than we know ourselves.

Writers who discover their own topics write with voice and commitment. It is these qualities that draw us to the writing and make us care what the writer has to say. When the voice is strong, the writing literally becomes an extension of self. We trust a writer with strong voice to be telling the truth. Through this trust, voice builds a bond from writer to reader. And because writing with voice is worth reading, we should do everything possible to encourage students to create such writing, and everything we can think of to eliminate time wasted on creating writing no one—writer or reader—cares about. Caring is everything. Anne Lamott says it best: "My gratitude for good writing is unbounded; I'm grateful for it the way I'm grateful for the ocean" (1995, 15).

Finding personally important topics is not as simple as it might sound. Students who have not had practice selecting their own topics may feel abandoned and adrift when asked to do so. My colleague Steve Kramer asked his fourth graders this question: *What is the hardest thing about writing?* As you can see from their answers, many of them zeroed right in on topic selection:

The Hardest Thing About Writing

- The hardest thing about writing is trying to find a topic about what to write and if it would sound good.
- It is hard for me to write because it is stressful.

- You can never put in all the details you want. It would take ages.
- The hardest thing about writing is thinking what to write and spelling.
- The hardest thing about writing for me is to consintrat.
- The hardest thing about writing is having to think about what you are going to write.
- It's getting the words in the right place and starting your pharagranf.
- The hardest part is when you run out of ideas.
- It's when you get stuck and don't know what to write about.
- The hardest part is to think what you will write.
- Thinking about what you are going to write.
- Figering out how to begin.
- You have to spell crecktly. And you have to think a lot.
- It's holding your thoughts for one book until you are done with another one.
- Writing about the topic you chose.
- Thinking what to write, but that's why I like it.

 As writing coaches, we have to help students—not by choosing for them, but by helping them learn to choose for themselves. Independence is a tricky thing. We don't want to push our students off a cliff. That's what we do, in effect, when we say, "Go ahead—write about anything that interests you." If we teach them to hang glide, and provide the necessary equipment (and confidence), they'll leap from the cliff themselves. Where to begin?

First, many students have not thought deeply about purposes for writing, and may not have a good understanding of the differences among story, essay, memoir, research writing, technical and informational writing, business writing, and argument (or persuasive writing). It helps to define these various forms, and to talk about purpose. Sometimes, the purposes overlap. For example, in *My War*, Andy Rooney shuns a textbook approach, combining research with memoir for reasons he makes clear on the very first page:

> I attended a symposium of distinguished historians in Chicago in 1994. Some of them were in their sixties, marginally too young to have served in World War II. I was in awe of their intellectuality until they started lecturing specifically about the war I knew. If you break your leg and go to a doctor who knows all about broken legs

but has never broken his own, you know just a little bit about broken legs that the doctor does not. I thought about that listening to the historians. They had read and studied about the war for years and had a great grasp of the overall picture. There was only one advantage I had over all of them. I was there when it happened. (2000, 3)

Sharing examples like this one helps students understand that memoir is a little different from straight history, that memory and experience can enrich research. His personal involvement in the war allows Rooney to write about his visit to the concentration camp at Thekla in a way that shows the significance of a tiny detail someone who hadn't been there might not know of or think about:

> In half a dozen places on the bare wooden walls next to the tier of bunks up against it, the prisoners had scratched out squares for chessboards. Pinned to the squares were crude paper cutouts of chessmen. There was no good reason to feel any worse about the death of a man with a brain active enough to want to play chess under those circumstances but, nonetheless, I could not resist thinking that it was worse. (269)

Samples inspire us, remind us of details or images that might otherwise be lost, and also awaken us to the inherent appeal of an unexpected approach. As the preceding example shows, to Andy Rooney history and memoir are extraordinarily compatible.

In her stunning book *Hoofprints: Horse Poems*, Jessie Haas blends history with poetry, tracing the evolution of the horse through a panorama of images all spinning toward the inevitable connection of horse and rider. This early example takes us back to the very beginning of the saga:

How the World Makes Horses

She drives the continents apart.
She heats and wets and dries and cools the land,
Makes winter, summer, rainfall, grass.
Then out of a nub of guinea pig-like flesh
She spins her long fantastic thread,
Pulling and twisting and whirling.
She sets up land-bridges,
Spills her animals across,
Walls them behind ice,

Islands them, and isthmuses, and peninsulas them,
And reconnects when they are stubby ponies
Or tall dry desert runners;
Combines the separate kinds she has created,
Throws away ninety-five percent,
Preserves the remnant on a whim,
And twines them at last with the human-thread
She has been simultaneously spinning
To create a two-ply
Of considerable strength. (2004, 10)

Second, we need to focus on students themselves. After all, writing springs from who we are. When students say they have nothing to write about, they are really saying in effect, "I'm not a very interesting person. My life is dull. I'm dull." It isn't true, but if they *think* it's true, the result is the same. Students often think we read their writing only to see how good it is. The notion that we might read it to learn something or to appreciate the voice or the language never occurs to many of them. Our sincere interest in students' lives and their opinions is one of the strongest motivators we have. Nothing on earth is so irresistible to a writer as the knowledge that her writing might actually influence someone else's thoughts or feelings. And if that is not true, there is no compelling reason to write. We cannot coerce nonwriters into writing. We can only coax them by promising the one thing no writer can resist: an appreciative audience.

Third, we need to talk *honestly* about where ideas come from. Ideas are all around us, swarming, overwhelming us. Every book, film, conversation, ride on the bus, glance out the window sparks a hundred possibilities for writing—if you have learned to think like a writer. If not, the whole world looks like a blank page. Stephen King puts it bluntly:

Let's get one thing clear right now, shall we? There is no Idea Dump no Story Central, no Island of the Buried Bestsellers; good story ideas seem to come quite literally from nowhere, sailing at you right out of the empty sky: two previously unrelated ideas come together and make something new under the sun. Your job isn't to find these ideas but to recognize them when they show up. (2000, 37)

In the aftermath of 2004's Hurricane Frances, I learned from a friend who lives in Fort Lauderdale what it is to live without electricity or running water for three days, and how difficult it is to sit in the darkness created by the essential hurricane shutters you must close over your windows. At the end of three days, people were desperate for light, and those who lived alone longed to hear a human voice that did not come from a radio. They braved floods, out-of-order traffic lights, and downed power lines to travel to the one corner tavern that was open, where a generator operated a small neon sign in the window, a sign no one would have noticed three days prior, a sign that had now become a beacon of salvation. Humans crave conversation, and will sometimes risk their lives for it. Even nondrinkers flocked to the tavern, sharing with strangers their stories of harrowing escapes and rescues. This image of Fort Lauderdale residents huddled in the glow of the tavern light is one of those details that makes its way deep into the imagination. It's part of my own memory now, and when the moment is right, it will be there for me, waiting to be woven into some larger piece.

Writers gather, store, and save. Novelist Richard Peck describes the process this way:

> We get our ideas from memories, usually of other people, even other people's memories. And from other people's books. We're always looking to other people for our stories, then creating other people to tell them.
> For me, writing a novel is like making a quilt. You gather bright scraps from other people's lives, and then you stitch them together in a pattern of your own. (2002, 73)

Ideas also come from observation. But we must teach ourselves, and our students, to sit up and take notice. To be aware of the world around us. To sift through our experience for those ideas that are worth preserving or developing through writing. Kathleen Dean Moore, a professor of philosophy at Oregon State University, has written a remarkable book on reflective thinking called *Riverwalking: Reflections on Moving Water*. Among other philosophical musings, Moore talks about the many benefits of "poking around"—simply investigating the world and storing in our minds what we find there:

> Poking around is a guaranteed way to learn. Ideas, after all, start with sense impressions; and all learning comes from making connections among observations and ideas. Insight is born of analogy. Everything interesting is complicated. Since truth is in the details, seekers of the truth should look for it there. (1995, 36)

We are, Moore tells us, like curators in walking, living, breathing museums: ourselves. We collect impressions, images, memories: "Every time you notice something, every time something strikes you as important enough to store away in your mind, you create another piece of who you are" (36). So when the well runs dry, when students complain there is nothing to write about, it may be they just need to poke around a bit more. Perhaps poking around should be a major focus of our writing curriculum, for nothing is so essential to a writer's independence and success as the ability to find personally important topics.

And as we are poking around, another writer's habit we would do well to cultivate is to write down what we see or notice or think about. Writers often keep journals for this very reason. And what to put in this journal? Oh, anything and everything. As Katie Wood Ray tells us, a writer's journal may hold "an interesting tidbit we've overheard, a question that's just occurred to us, a fascinating play of light on oil on water in our driveway. Anything. We just write it down. We never know what might come of it, and we have to get some ideas, some material we can work with in our writing" (2002, 33).

It is often wise to begin our search for topics close to home. Donald Murray reminds us that to be effective, a writer must "be an author—an authority" (2004, 96) on his or her subject. What we know best is ourselves, our families, the most vivid memories, places, times, smells, and sounds of our childhood. I am comfortable writing about my mother playing chicken with a truck driver in Montana because she did not want her new Pontiac sprayed with gravel. I am an authority on that story because I was there, riding with her.

I was also there when my Uncle Gus wrestled an eight-foot blue spruce up the three flights of his apartment building because Aunt Elva needed a sturdy tree on which to display her heavy, handmade Christmas ornaments. I stood on tiptoe, three flights up, peering down the open stairwell, listening to the echoes against the brick and concrete walls. I can picture Gus forcing those resistant, stubborn branches through the downstairs door, then pressing himself hard against the wall, only his black boots poking out, to let another (very impatient) resident squeeze by. I can smell the scent of the freshly cut tree mingling with the aroma of baked cookies. Against the background of Perry Como singing "(There's No Place Like) Home for the Holidays" I hear the scraping of branches, my uncle's muffled curses, the thunk of the heavy tree trunk announcing each landing, and the click of Aunt Elva's three-inch high heels on the linoleum floor as she came to open the door and ask Gus what in God's name had taken him so long to bring in a simple Christmas tree. I was there when I was ten, and I will be there forever because I remember.

In modeling topic selection for your students, start by thinking, "I know this because I was there." Make a list. From this personal beginning, think of possible writing topics going out in circles, like ripples around a stone in the water. Beyond ourselves and our families come things like school and community, then the city or other personal geography that's familiar, along with the culture we know. Beyond that lies the larger world of diverse communities and cultures, distant, but still observable. And beyond that, the less observable worlds of philosophy, history, anthropology, and physical science. The farther out we go, the more research we need to become the authorities Donald Murray tells us we must be to write with authenticity and voice.

Sometimes topics seem to find us. They reach out and grab us. Laura Hillenbrand, author of *Seabiscuit*, tells how the idea for her famous book came to her through some very casual reading:

> In 1996, I was going through some old racing material when I came across a few bits of information on Seabiscuit's jockey, owner, and trainer. It struck me as fascinating that an automobile magnate who had devoted his life to making horses obsolete would find his greatest success in managing a racehorse with a frontier horseman. I was intrigued enough to look a little deeper. I quickly realized that I had found an extraordinarily dramatic human story to go with the equine one. I spent the next four years researching it. (*The New York Times*, September 3, 2003)

Hillenbrand's research took her to record books and interviews, films and photographs. "I researched what things cost, what books and movies were popular, what the weather was on a particular day, anything that might help me stand in the shoes of an average American of the Depression era." This writer's commitment to research allows us to turn to any page of the book and feel as if we are going back in time. Her extraordinary knowledge of her topic, and everything related to it, turned the simple story of a horse into a mesmerizing slice of history. Knowing a topic well is the foundation of voice.

Some people spend their whole lives immersed in research and become as much at home with the most distant star as you or I might feel sitting on the porch swing. That's why someone like Carl Sagan writes about the cosmos with such heart:

> The earth is a place. It is by no means the only place. It is not even a typical place. No planet or star or galaxy can be typical, because the Cosmos is mostly empty. The only typical place is within the vast, cold, universal vacuum, the everlasting night of intergalactic space, a place so strange and desolate that, by comparison, planets and stars and galaxies seem achingly rare and lovely. (1980, 5)

If you think about it even briefly, chances are you will readily identify the salient topics of your own life, those things to which you return again and again, like treasures kept in a special box. For Laura Hillenbrand, horses hold a special fascination. Charles Kuralt's passion was travel. Diane Ackerman loves science and gardening, while a part of Gary Paulsen's heart will forever be in the Alaskan wilderness, running with his beloved dogs. But what of our students? Have they lived long enough to develop passions like these?

This is not a simple question to answer. Everyone, even a toddler, has writing-worthy moments. Everyone has topics that touch his or her heart. It takes time and practice, however, to become skilled at identifying these moments and topics that will probably live with us forever. In the course of the search, some of our student writers are likely to get frustrated. That's when it's tempting to just give in and tell them what to write about. After all, won't this save them a lot of time and trouble? Absolutely. But then, the opportunity to teach real thinking is lost.

In a refreshingly honest book called *Confessions of a Slacker Mom*, Muffy Mead-Ferro talks about the difficulty of resisting the temptation to buy one's child every new, educational, or technologically superior toy. The problem is, she says, the toys do all the work: They set the rules, play the music, make the images, keep the child coloring within the lines. Moreover, such toys hold children's attention only for a limited time since there is no imaginative investment on the part of the child. Mead-Ferro's own children, by contrast, have frequently made toys out of things that do not come packaged or labeled: sticks, tires, rocks and trees to climb, stones to throw in the river, an old cardboard box turned into a fort. They've had to be inventive. Her reasons are simple: "I'd rather they learn creative thinking. That will allow them to entertain themselves and solve their own problems. And maybe even exit childhood with some of the tools they'll need to be independent adults responsible for their own success and happiness" (2004, 31–32).

Similarly, independent writers must take responsibility for finding their own topics. Like parents who shower their children with too many toys, we pay a heavy price for caving in to writing shortcuts: lack of motivation, voiceless writing, even a growing sense (among some students) that they simply cannot write. "When we give the topic to our students," Donald Murray tells us, "we assume a common experience that does not exist" (2004, 96). We assume both knowledge and interest because *we* have knowledge and interest. The students, though, may have neither, and may think that having neither is their fault.

The truth is, the only person to whom I can assign topics effectively is myself. Just because I enjoy writing about oversized Christmas trees or games of chicken on the back roads of Montana is no sign you will, or that my students would. Perhaps you think cloning, stem cell research, and global warming are topics of significant interest about which everyone should have an opinion. Your students might rather explore the history of jazz or the controversial use of drugs in sports or ecologists' efforts to reinstate wolves in Idaho. When we suggest a topic that doesn't push the right button, students may think, "If you find that so interesting, why don't *you* write about it?"

Maybe we should. We could occasionally invite students to assign *us* a topic, then write on it, right in front of them—on the overhead, perhaps. That way, they can see how a writer begins dealing with a topic that did not spring from her own imagination. They can also see (and we can feel, as we write) how hard it is to put voice into assigned writing. Student writers need to see us struggle because that's what writing is, mostly. Writing is hard. It can also change, overnight—right there in the file drawer. What sounded pretty good yesterday often transmogrifies into something every bit as dreadful as you feared it might be when you woke up thinking about it last night. If you throw it away and start over, you may find yourself staring at the blank screen or paper with nothing, not one blooming word, coming into your head.

That's the moment of deepest, darkest temptation, the moment that makes a dieter reach for a chocolate and a writer reach for a chocolate *and* a prompt: "OK, enough with the soul searching. Where's Mr. Graphite when we need him?" Assignments can be ugly, yes, but they have real parameters, and they don't leave us floating in "the everlasting night of intergalactic space" where writers live so much of the time.

Students look to us for writing ideas not because we inspire them, but because it is easier to follow an assignment than to think on your own what you will write. That is precisely why it is so important for writers—all writers—to do so. Defining a topic is central to the thinking part of writing. There are only two reasons, really, to define a topic *for* students: (1) the content (*history of ballet, evolution of the horse*) is just as important as the quality of writing itself, and is not up for negotiation; or (2) the general domain of knowledge (*psychoanalysis*) is new to students, and so defining a specific topic within that domain will be difficult for a novice, and calls for a little help.

Generally speaking, neither situation is true in a large-scale writing assessment, yet we persist in defining topics for our students, thereby dismissing the very thing we should care about most: the writer's ability to think like a writer. Imagine. If we allowed students in assessment situations to define their own topics, their skill in doing so could become part of what we assess, thereby literally doubling the significance of that assessment. We would eliminate concerns and complaints about stupid or inappropriate prompts. Best of all, from the readers' point of view, we would eliminate the tedium of having to read five thousand papers on "A Day I'll Always Remember."

"Inconsistency!" someone is screaming from stage left. You bet. A very real and present danger if we allow students to write about any old thing that interests them—but also, ironically, a benefit. In writing, inconsistency goes by many other names: originality, individuality, variance, new perspective, risk. All of which lead to voice. And all of which we forego when we say, "Look here, I am very busy, and I want to skim through these papers quickly and notice that whereas Carlos has given me *five* sensory details about his special day, Joan has shared only *three*." It is cowardly and presumptuous for us to assume that left to their own devices, Carlos will not come up with a topic as interesting as Nephila, the golden silk spider, or that Joan won't have enough imagination to take us right inside her favorite restaurant, seat us in the corner booth, and make us wish we could meet there every Friday night. Think of the places we might go as readers if we dared to trust just a little.

In the classroom, trust comes easier. We are rarely bound by someone else's assignment. We can help Joan and Carlos become thinkers, not just responders, and with that, creators of literature. We can grant ourselves as readers the gift of surprise. Forty years from now, perhaps one of our students will open a desk drawer, pull out a piece of writing from long ago, and say, "Here— read this. I wrote it in tenth grade and saved it all this time."

FROM A WRITER'S NOTEBOOK

School Rules

TOM NEWKIRK

The local newspaper has been filled recently with stories about a censorship attempt at a Maine high school concerning *Catcher in the Rye*, which after forty years can still offend parents with its language. One school board member came out in favor of the ban because it was not consistent to allow Holden to use language that would be inappropriate in the school.

At a local elementary school, the principal explained the "no violence in writing" policy, common to many schools in this post-Columbine era. Students, she explained, cannot include in their stories action that would be forbidden in the school.

For a moment, I fantasized about a large assembly, convened to explain this new rule. It would be attended not only by student writers, but by published writers and by the characters they created. Seated in the auditorium would be fighter pilots from the first graders' war stories, serial killers from horror stories, vampire slayers, gothic warriors, and a few man-eating plants. Darth Vader would be sitting next to the BFG and Hamlet. At the back of the auditorium would be a row of slouching monsters. Beowulf's nemesis, Grendel, too big to fit inside, would be looking in a window.

Some major school official would explain to the assembly that from now on the student behavior code will apply to them. They are to "use words" to solve their disputes; they are to respect each other; and to leave weapons at home. They should look at themselves as "role models." Should they persist in violent conflict, they will have to attend compulsory counseling sessions focusing on anger management.

When these restrictions are applied to literature, anticensorship groups rise to challenge them (as they have in the Maine incident). But when applied to student writing, there is a deafening silence. Presumably it is acceptable, even artistic, for Beowulf to pull off Grendel's arm, but inappropriate, or grounds for clinical referral, if boys play around with similar fantasies.

I'm suspicious of anyone my age appealing to the golden age of our youth. Memory and nostalgia distort far too much. But I do think some forms of male fantasy play were more accepted as normal then. To check this perception, I called my mother, now ninety-two. When I told her I was writing about boys and violence, she hesitated, then said reluctantly, "I suppose you are going to tell the story about the Easter basket."

"Mom, what Easter basket?"

"Well, you remember when you were a kid how you were allergic to chocolate, so we couldn't put the regular candy in your basket. We didn't want you to go without so we gave you a toy gun."

"Mom, you put a toy *gun* in my Easter basket?"

"Yeah. We didn't want you to go without. It seemed OK back then."

We all collected the regular arsenal—six-shooters, cap pistols, and squirt guns of various sizes. We played with them, but never, I firmly believe, confused what we were doing with real warfare. In fact, I grew up to be a conscientious objector to war.

The prohibitions now in place in many elementary schools will not eliminate the need for these fantasies of power and conflict. They will not transform human nature so that it is no longer interested in the extremes of human experience. They will just drive this fascination outside the classroom—and make school less relevant to human needs.

THOMAS NEWKIRK *teaches at the University of New Hampshire where he established and continues to direct the New Hampshire Literacy Institute. He is the author of* Misreading Masculinity: Boys, Literacy, and Popular Culture *and* The Performance of Self in Student Writing, *which won the David Russell Award from the National Council of Teachers of English.*

Three
The Right to Go "Off Topic"

Some years ago, following a state writing assessment, a teacher approached me with a piece of student writing about which she had concerns. "I am just wondering if this was scored correctly," she said. When people ask me to respond to a piece of writing, I try to approach it with as little extraneous information as possible because so many things *other* than the quality of the writing, the thing we should be focusing on, can influence our thinking. So, I did not ask her what scores the piece had received or even why she was asking me to review it. I just read it.

Writing a first draft is very much like watching a Polaroid develop. You can't—and, in fact, you're not supposed to—know exactly what the picture is going to look like until it has finished developing.

—ANNE LAMOTT
Writing Changes Everything
ed. Deborah Brodie

The essay was about two then-endangered species, the southern sea otter and the caribou, what the government was doing to protect them, and what citizens should do as well. The writing was thoughtful, expansive, and well-organized, filled with explicit detail about what each animal needed to survive. The writer made a strong case for the uniqueness of each creature's habitat, and depicted its place in a larger environmental chain. She made me feel the potential impact of losing even one endangered species, and the price we might pay for our indifference.

"How would *you* score this paper?" the teacher asked, and I responded truthfully that I would give it very high scores, for it was clear, passionate, and organized—in short, just what I look for in any piece of writing, not just students' writing. I was amazed, frankly, as I commented to this teacher, that such a piece had come out of a writing assessment, where I knew the time had been limited and students had had no access (once testing began) to resources that could provide a knowledge base for such writing. This student had pulled a wealth of information out of her head, and had written a cogent, compelling argument calling for the protection of two animals she clearly cared about. Moreover, she had managed all this in less than an hour's time, with no previous knowledge of what she would be asked. By any reasonable writing standards we might set, this had been a stellar performance. A knockout. This student had accomplished what many adult writers could not. The appropriate response? That should be an easy one. Why would there be any question?

The teacher nodded as if I had validated her deepest conviction. Just out of curiosity I asked her what the prompt had been. With that, I pulled the cork out of the dam. "That's just the trouble," she told me. "The prompt asked students to write about one endangered species." I nodded. I still didn't get it. "Well," she coached me, "she wrote about *two. Two* species, don't you see? She went *off topic.* That's why she received a score of 1—out of a possible 5. And we're just wondering, some of us, if that's fair or not. Look—I have a whole stack of them here—students who wrote about two animals instead of one." And indeed she held a stack of forty or so papers, all written by students who, in their eagerness to tell the world just how important it is to care for our wildlife, had written about two endangered creatures, not just one as the prompt had specified.

Let's leave that teacher with her stack of papers for a minute. We'll come back, I promise.

This is not an isolated incident. Repeatedly, I have seen scorers for district or state writing assessments dissolve into a veritable frenzy because student writers seemed to drift from the topic. Just wander off, as if without regard for the prompt. How dare they? Sometimes, a student truly does write about something completely apart from the question asked, almost as if he or she hadn't read the prompt at all. The prompt might ask what is required to be a good leader, for example, and the student writes about fishing in Maine with Uncle Jake. We could try inferring that Uncle Jake has leadership potential or that fishermen make the best leaders—and both might be true. It is an inference, though. Other times, as in the example I've just recounted, the prompt is interpreted so literally by readers that the slightest deviation from what is requested causes scores to plummet, sometimes mercilessly. What is so insidious about this off-topic response to student writing is that it looks so appropriate, so justified, so—*helpful.* The reader-responder may be saying in his or her mind, "It's difficult to stay on track when you write, so let me help you out by keeping my eagle eye upon you, noting when you wander, even a tad, and zapping you with a low score, so that in future you will remember to write about the prompt, the whole prompt, and nothing but the prompt, so help you God."

There are a number of things wrong with this approach.

First, it's open to interpretation. What *is* off topic anyway? Even if I were a fan of the off topic label (which anyone who knows me knows I am not), I would not regard the two-species-versus-one paper a qualified candidate. The writer expanded the topic a bit, true. Good for her. She knew more than the prompt required. She did not, however, address women's rights or the European market. She was very focused in her argument and gave back more than the prompt writers had any right to hope for. We should applaud this kind of writing, not trivialize the writer's gift to us with lower scores.

Second, the off topic label assumes a certain "prompt nobility" that simply does not exist. If you were to make a list of the loftier sorts of writing in which a person can engage and the humbler sorts, what might you put on each list? On my lofty list, I would include things like poetry, song lyrics, a good travel book or memoir, any novel with fine dialogue, research-based writing with voice, and young children's letters to their parents or teachers. Among the humbler writing samples I would include most government documents, political speeches, form letters of all types, any writing that incorporates kute spelling, and prompts.

Not that prompt writers do not try to make prompts interesting. It simply is not possible to come up with one writing topic that fits all. You have to consider age, gender, culture, and experience. Not every child has had a pet, for example, and so "Describe your most exotic pet" becomes the elusive, hypothetical "Think of an animal you would like to have as a pet, and make up a story about one day you spent together." This is the sort of floaty conjecturing that leads to voiceless writing: *My pet was a boa constrictor named Lucky. I kept him in a cage in my bedroom. One day he escaped and I looked for him all day. I finally found him under my sister's bed. She screamed, but Lucky was sound asleep.* (Digesting a prompt writer, perhaps. Can't hurt to hope.)

"Why don't students put more voice into their writing?" we ask. Why don't caged animals run more? Writers trying to assume a passion they do not feel for a topic they did not think up should not be expected to kick the voice level above "earnest." It's not fair. Further, since we know what the problem is, we should not only allow students to wander far afield from these banal topics, we should encourage it. Our attitude should be, "If you can come up with a better idea (and oh, how we hope you can), go for it." It's arrogant to assume that we can come up with better topics for our student writers than they can think up for themselves. And even if we could, they need the opportunity to seek out those personal topics, for that is one cornerstone of good writing.

Writers who write about what matters to them write with a natural voice. They do not have to put it on like a suit coat. I can borrow a voice for any topic in the world: *Ah, the majesty of elephants . . .* or, *Who knew geometry had the power to rock the world . . .* or, *Economics has much in common with a well-written mystery novel, except we may never find out who done it . . .* This off-the-rack voice never has quite the power of homespun, however. For a custom fit, you need a customized topic.

I can see some eyebrows going up. I can hear voices saying, "But sometimes, we *want* students to write about a particular topic, for a particular purpose." Yes, that is true. It is true when we want to measure what students *know*. This is sometimes true in the classroom where writing is used as a way of gauging understanding of a topic or whole field of study—geometry, twentieth-century events, wildlife management. Even so, it is a rare teacher who cannot be flexible about the chosen topic within certain parameters. If a teacher is seeking an answer to a very narrowly defined question, then "Explain the process by which paper is made" probably cannot be modified much. But if the purpose is to explore a broader concept—say the Vietnam conflict—then any number of narrowed topics will do. We encourage thinking when we ask students to pose and answer their own questions. Oh, writer, prompt thyself.

In large-scale assessment, the purpose is different. Content is of little consequence if we are measuring how well students can *write* because a writer can demonstrate skill while writing about any topic whatsoever. Unfortunately, we are not always crystal clear (even in the best assessments) about what our purpose is—or to put it another way, what it is we wish to find out. This lack of clarity gets us into trouble, every time. Good assessment begins with an unambiguous answer to the question *What, precisely, do we want to know?* In the case of writing, we must often choose between content knowledge and writing skill. Sometimes we get both, but asking for both when we are pretending to ask for only one is not fair. In assigning any prompt, we need to look closely at the standards or criteria by which the writing will be judged and ask, "Will this prompt encourage writing in which the writer can demonstrate the required skills?" What a simple, logical thing to do. Yet it does not always happen.

Third, we should acknowledge (Why do we fight this?) that prompts, by their very nature, tend to elicit dull writing from all but the most determined and energetic responders. In large-scale assessment, because a single prompt (or sometimes, a choice of two) must be suitable to so many writers, we do not ask questions for which we are really, truly, deeply interested in the answer. That is part of the problem. Interesting, provocative questions are things like, *If you could change your GPA with a keystroke, would you do it? What do you wish your parents understood about you? Have you ever disliked someone intensely, and if so, why? Is it all right to lie sometimes? Can you describe the first moment you fell in love? What were you thinking during your first kiss? What frightens you?* Questions like these are intriguing, but also personal, intrusive, and totally inappropriate for a writing assessment. Prompt writers work hard not to step on toes, become too nosey, or ask questions that are likely to provoke disturbing answers. That is fair—and right. But we must also then allow students to tinker a bit if they wish to personalize a prompt. And we do need to encourage them to personalize writing topics. Personalizing, even when it shapes a response in a way that a prompt writer, assessor, or teacher could not have imagined, is not a fault. It is one of the true secrets of great writing. We must also acknowledge that coming up with a brilliant and thought-provoking answer to an inherently dull question is more than we have any right to ask of our student writers. Few of us could do it. In any assessment, student writers who rise above the prompt create the most expressive, thoughtful, and readable writing.

A fourth problem with the off topic issue is that it causes us to assess the simple thing, not the important thing. It turns writing assessment into a control issue: *Wander from my topic and you will pay.* We get so hung up on looking at whether writers have precisely addressed a question we cared little about in the first place (the easy thing to assess) that we forget to look at the quality of the writing (the hard thing). If we really wish to test students' ability (or really, willingness) to follow directions precisely, there are many more efficient and economical ways to do it than through writing assessment. The bigger issue here, though, is whether following directions matters all that much. If I were teaching math, biology, or driver's education, following directions would matter to me enormously. Even if I were teaching golf or pool or poker, directions would matter. The way you hold a golf club affects your swing and so, the whole game, not to mention any windows within your range. Similarly, a full house cannot *sometimes* beat three of a kind and sometimes not. In writing, though, creativity matters. Spontaneity is a virtue. Originality and perspective define voice. Risk is essential to success. And writers who never think for themselves cannot get anywhere. If I try to control your writing, I will never get the best you have to give—nor do I deserve it.

Consider this example from Garrison Keillor, who is the master of going off the apparent topic and onto the *real* topic—which in turn becomes a stepping stone for the topic after that. Keillor leapfrogs from one lily pad to another, but the leaping is not so random as it looks. There is always a connection. We must read carefully to see it, though, and I do not envision much of Keillor's writing passing unbruised through the portals of formalized scoring. In his Introduction to *Leaving Home*, Keillor talks about the sense of smell, a train of thought prompted by his lying in bed under an old family quilt, which carries aromas that take him back to his childhood:

> We have so much language to describe how things sound and look—and so few words for how things smell and feel to our touch, our animal senses—so a smart guy like me thinks he can give up smell for the pleasure of smoking. Tobacco smoke overpowers and deadens about two-thirds of a smoker's sense of smell, and a few

days after I stopped, I began to notice the vast realm of smells that were lost all those years. (1987, xvii)

Keillor then spends a full page recounting the smells he experiences through his renewed sensory awareness—smells of food and old garages and people—as well as all the associations that accompany them. And from the smell of fried potatoes on the stove and newly cut grass he leapfrogs to this story:

> When I was four years old, I fell through a hole in the haymow into the bull pen, missing the stanchion and landing in his feed trough full of hay, and was carried into the house and laid on my grandma's sofa, which smelled like this quilt, and so did a warm shirt handed down to me from my uncle. When I was little I didn't think of grownups as having bare skin; grownups were made of wool clothing, only kids were bare-naked; now I'm older than they were when I was little and I lie naked under a quilt made of their clothes when they were children. I don't know what makes me think I'm smarter than them. (xviii–xix)

For anyone who values formulaic writing, this sort of text is a virtual nightmare. I can hear in my head a traditional scorer's response to this piece: "Well, look—he begins here with the language we use to describe different senses. Then we're into the advantages of quitting smoking, but instead of developing that topic, the writer launches into a long list of smells ranging from food to garages. We shift here from expository to narrative writing, with this story about falling in the bull pen, which is never finished, by the way. What happened after they laid him on the couch? What happened to the bull, for that matter? Then there's a sudden shift here to this comment about grown-ups being made of wool clothing—whatever that means—and a very abrupt ending that doesn't connect to anything at all. The fellow has some voice, to be sure, but no real sense of organization. And almost none of these various ideas are developed. He also uses a few too many semicolons for my taste. What was the prompt here again?"

When we read in a different way, not looking for an implanted outline, not obsessed with making connections to a prompt, we read with understanding, and we see the point the writer is really trying to make: that a familiar smell (say, of a quilt) can take you back, just like *that*, to your earliest childhood, and suddenly there you are, comparing the child that you once were to the adult you are now. Once you thought you were smart and your life would be different, oh, so different from theirs, but now *you* know that the things they experienced in life, you will experience, too. The quilt made from their clothing is also the fabric of your life.

This piece wasn't really about language or smoking or garages or falling into the bull pen, after all. Those were just stepping stones (lily pads) along the path to a deeper truth: that life is short indeed, and once you are looking at your life from the far side of time, something so fragile as the scent of a quilt will bind you to the memory of the child you were just moments ago. Keillor trusts us to get the meaning without his having to be too literal. We trust him to leapfrog to the points that matter.

Not all writers are as skilled as Keillor. True. But the point is that where the writer begins is not always where he or she needs to wind up. A prompt's highest and best use is as a beginning for the thinking that follows. Keillor does not wander randomly. He has something to say—about the link between smell and memory, and the link between memory and a growing sense of who we are. We have a right to ask that student writers make a point in their writing, too. That's fair. Sometimes, though, they must travel a bit from the prompt to get there. That can be a very good thing, for sometimes they take us along on a journey of thought that goes well beyond the horizon we see when we stand in the center of that prompt and look out.

We should also be careful not to give students the idea that all writing is prompt-connected. "What was the prompt?" is rarely a helpful question to ask. Notice that we do *not* say about newspaper articles or essays in *Time* magazine, "Well, if I knew what the editor had *assigned*, I'd understand this better." Certainly we do not ask it about novels or biographies, poems or social commentary. We do ask, "What is the theme?" or "What point is the writer trying to make?" These are good questions, for they go to the thought behind the writing, versus the assignment, which is artificial and superimposed. We should teach students that writing is successful not when it responds to the prompt in a literal, confined, and unimaginative way, but when it stands on its own, so that a reader doesn't need to know the assignment or prompt in order for the message to make sense.

Finally, obsession with the off topic concept shows a profound lack of understanding about the way writing works. Excluding those times when a writer is asked to or must address a specific question (*Explain your goals as a graduate student in psychology*), writers do not wander off topic, but rather *onto* their real topics.

Some years ago, I spent time as a reporter for the *Willamette Week* paper in Portland. During that time, I wrote a number of articles pertaining to health issues, one being weight loss. For the article I interviewed several people who had lost significant amounts of weight (one hundred pounds or more), and my original intention was to build the article around their strategies. What I discovered through my interviews, however, was that losing a large amount of weight can change a person not only physically, but emotionally and psychologically as well. People may become more confident following such weight loss, and sometimes more assertive as well. One change may lead to another: divorce or marriage, a move, a career shift, enrollment in college, the decision to buy a dog. For one woman I interviewed, it had just the opposite effect. She became very shy and withdrawn as a thin person, as if she had been protected by her previously larger physical presence and now felt vulnerable. Moreover, her friends related to her differently, as though she were no longer the person she had been. These emotional and social changes (some of which surprised me) soon became the focal point, the center of my writing, and I wound up having little to say about weight loss strategies. That article was reprinted in several places around the country, and pulled in more letters from readers than any other single thing I wrote while working for the paper.

Such shifts can occur even in much shorter pieces. In a writing group once we decided to do sensory detail pieces on places we could go out and experience firsthand. I decided to write about the school baseball field in the spring, and so began routinely attending the warm-ups, where I could take in all the sensory information I wanted to include in my writing. I sat at the very top of the old, hard, rickety bleachers, where I could take in the whole field, and that is where my writing began—with the feel of the wood, the smell of the grass, the sound of the baseballs hitting leather. I dutifully recorded all these impressions in my writer's notebook, but my attention shifted repeatedly to the pitcher, whose walk and style were so distinctive. I loved the way he eased up to the mound, the way he scuffed it with his toes, as if the last pitcher had left it a bit untidy. It reminded me of myself fluffing sofa pillows, or rearranging family pictures. I loved the way his whole body moved in the windup, every muscle part of one coordinated effort. Only his eyes never wandered. His focus was relentless. And it was as if he could see a target invisible to others, one tiny spot where that ball needed to go.

My appreciation for the pitcher's skill grew each day, and he became the center of the piece I eventually wrote. When I saw him talking to the coach, saw the way the coach's eyes followed the windup and the stretch, that little conversation by the mound—of which I heard not one word—made me imagine that the coach had once been a pitcher, too, and a story began to form in my head. That's how writing goes. Each little piece on the page opens a door beyond which is a fork in the road. There the writer can take the well-worn path, or the less-traveled road. We tend to reward the writers who travel the well-worn path, the expected route. We ought not to do this. If we truly believe that writing is thinking, then we must let our writers go where their thinking leads them—and as far as it will take them, even if that means leaving the best of our prompts far, far behind.

Remember the teacher with the stack of forty papers? We rescored them all. None of them received scores of 1 (on a 5-point scale) in "idea development." Most, in fact, received—and deserved—very high scores. It felt good to make that change. It was the right thing to do, and put us educationally back on track.

It did not, however, resolve the bigger problem, the need so many assessors feel to keep writers within the (sometimes) tight parameters of a topic. When we shackle writing with rigid prompts, we take over the ownership. If that is our intent, then why not just play *all* the parts? We could pose the prompts, write to them, and then score our own responses. Imagine the misunderstanding this could alleviate. After all, it is not fair to ask students to play the game with us unless we are willing to take their thinking seriously. What I would like to know is this: Were any of those papers on endangered species put to use? Sent to the Wildlife Bureau, published in the paper, assembled into a book, reviewed by the state legislature? If not, then it is only fair for students to say, "Guess what? I found a better question to answer."

FROM A WRITER'S NOTEBOOK

Help! I Need a Coach!

BOB ORNSTEIN

A good writing coach is hard to come by. Too many people will tell you your writing is good when it isn't, or they aren't sure what to tell you because in truth, they don't know whether the writing is good or what to do about it if it is not.

I didn't discover that my writing needed improvement until after I arrived in college. I thought I was a good writer. I had the grades and comments to prove it. My first college paper was for Professor Levine's class, Interpretations of American History. I recall the assignment vividly: Read *The Intellectual Origins of American Radicalism* and critique its thesis in a three-to-five-page essay. I was sure it would be easy.

I held this view because my high school writing assignments had been pushovers. In senior A. P. English, the capstone of high school writing, most assignments called for composing a single opening thesis paragraph or sentence instead of a full essay. We spent most of our time watching videos, not learning to write. Sure, we had a few longer assignments. I wrote a biography of Hemingway for which I made up my source material. *Oh, Hemingway!* was my favorite. To fill in, I copied verbatim from existing biographies. For my final project on Richard Wright, I showed my complete ignorance of Wright's historical and political significance by comparing, without a hint of irony, characters in *Native Son* to characters on *The Cosby Show*. The teacher never told me how inappropriate or misguided this comparison was.

My dad and I had regularly battled over my high school writing assignments, but his approach and relentless fixation on conventions left me feeling less than open to advice. He had been trained by demanding teachers, and was determined that I would learn the same way. It was a way that did not work for me. With his red pencil, he would meticulously correct everything—at least, everything I showed him. My inflated grades, combined with good standardized test scores, gave me the confidence to fight back. The correction sessions turned into awful arguments that exacerbated whatever father-son tensions already existed between us. I felt vindicated every time a teacher returned my paper (or paragraph) with high grades even though I had ignored the bulk of my father's suggestions.

At last though, the lack of challenging assignments and the absence of any really useful feedback was about to catch up with me. I was struggling. I even had trouble coming up with that magical first paragraph we had tried to perfect in A. P. English. I got so desperate I actually called my dad for help. "What is hegemony?" I remember futilely asking. Confused and worn out by what should have been a routine assignment, I desperately hammered together something I could hand in. And I finally got what I deserved. Professor Levine returned the paper a few days later with an F on the back page and a brief note: "See me."

Though I dreaded that meeting, it did not go as badly as I had expected. Mr. Levine began by asking me whether I had really tried. I told him I had made a huge effort, appearances notwithstanding. He gave me a hard look right then, and though I didn't know it at the time, I had found my first real writing coach.

Sitting with me in his book-lined office, Professor Levine began to show me that while my individual sentences made sense, they did not tie together. I had no vision of the whole piece. Despite all that "first paragraph" practice in high school, I had no thesis statement—but how could I? I had learned to write a thesis when someone handed me the subject. When I had to conceptualize it myself, I was stumped.

Mr. Levine showed me how to construct a rough outline covering my key points, and then have the essay flow from that skeleton. He didn't hover over me or delve into the particular details of grammar and word choice. He didn't pull out a red pen. Instead, he went straight to the internal thinking behind the writing. He showed me how to clarify my thoughts so I had a place to begin.

Armed with this second chance, I went back to the dorm and got to work. There I found my second coach, a perfect complement to Mr. Levine. My roommate, a self-professed stickler for conventions, helped me polish my drafts—when the time was right. I had, he told me, "no feeling whatever for comma placement." I redid that first essay twice, each time with feedback from Mr. Levine *and* my roommate. It was a real team effort. Over the course of the semester, through many assignments, I learned to write a cogent essay. I improved my sentence structure. And some commas began landing in the right places. By the end of the first year, I felt my writing was on par with that of most of my peers, and by the time I got my college degree, I felt I truly was a better writer. I knew what I was doing. When a teacher gave me a good grade, I felt I deserved it. When I got a low grade, I knew why.

My search for a writing coach taught me something important. From the beginning, Professor Levine's attention was more on my thinking than on the writing itself. Until then, everyone had either ignored the writing or the message—or had focused on spelling before I really had anything to say. Good coaching doesn't begin with spelling and grammar—or commas. It begins with the writer's ideas—and with the *writer*. Though I have learned to be my own coach now, I think it's important for every writer to have a Mr. Levine somewhere along the way.

BOB ORNSTEIN *lives with his soon-to-be-wife near San Francisco, California, where he works in marketing for a company called Invisalign. He plays as much tennis as possible not only for fun, but also to cope with the cost of living in the Bay Area. He enjoys writing silly emails to his brothers and friends, and still jokes with his college roommate about commas.*

Four

The Right to Personalize Writing Process

*T*wenty-first century writing instruction can and should take student writers toward independence—toward greater control over their writing and the process by which they create it. Such independence can occur only when process is personalized, shaped to fit the writer—because process at its best, at its most functional, is different for every person.

No two writers go about the business of discovering, shaping, or sharing ideas in just the same way, any more than they dance or speak or laugh or make love in the same way. Some writers rehearse an idea in their heads for hours or for months. Then, they fly through a draft as if guiding a kayak down the rapids. Most of the writing has already happened in their minds, and putting text on paper is only a way of formally recording thoughts. Other writers use the very act of writing to *do* their thinking. They revise as they go, constantly tinkering to make the words on the page match the thoughts in the mind, rewriting so much and so vigorously that they never actually create anything we could truly call a *rough* draft.

The writing process is an untidy business. In the years since Writing: Teachers and Children at Work *was published, I've found that some teachers have misunderstood the writing process. They deliberately take children through phases of making a choice, rehearsing, composing, and then rewriting. Of course, these processes do exist, but each child uses them differently. We simply cannot legislate their precise timing.*

—DONALD H. GRAVES
A Fresh Look at Writing

Some writers work on a piece steadily, day and night, till it is done, while others resign their early roughs to a state of dormancy for days, weeks, or even years. Given a choice, some writers would share everything they write with anyone who would listen; they live for feedback, and their confidence is unimpaired by the occasional inability of others to appreciate the genius behind their words. By contrast, some writers do not want anyone to see or hear a line prior to publication. They consider it bad luck—and an unpleasant experience to boot.

Thus, when we teach writing process, it's like preparing students for anything that's based on experience, such as traveling. Like traveling, writing is an elusive experience that comes in many guises, looks a little different just about every time you do it, is subject to the whims of fate (for *hurricanes* substitute *computer crashes*), and can never be precisely the same for any two people. We cannot prepare students for every eventuality of the writing journey, but we can provide them with some process fundamentals that will enable them to become independent travelers, to avoid many pitfalls, and to take themselves to destinations we cannot even envision.

In order for our students to become independent writers, several things must be in place. First, they need an environment in which process can flourish. Within this environment, they need to observe writing *in action* so they can begin to understand how process *can* work and *can* look. (Later, they can make personal adjustments.) At the same time, of course, they need to try it out for themselves. They need to *write*—extensively, expansively, frequently, and for varied purposes. And finally, they need a balance of structure and freedom, some things to depend on, and some to invent for themselves. Let's begin with the writing environment.

In *A Fresh Look at Writing*, Donald Graves makes the point that successful writing instruction is often less about *strategy* than about establishing the right *conditions* for writing (1994, 103). Writers need a classroom culture that supports writing, a culture in which everyone, including the teacher, is part of a writing community. They need a supportive environment in which they feel safe. Safe to try new things, to share their writing, to take risks, and to feel free from the compulsive need for perfection. "Perfectionism," writer and teacher Anne Lamott reminds us, "is the voice of the oppressor, the enemy of the people" (1995, 28). We need some clutter and mess when we write, for that's how writing in process looks. "Tidiness," Lamott says, "makes me think of held breath, of suspended animation, while writing needs to breathe and move" (29). In a supportive, nurturing environment, the *act of writing* always meets with approval and deep appreciation, even when the writing itself needs revision. In such an environment, everyone's writing experience and expertise are valued, and each person is both mentor and student.

Many of the conditions that nourish writing success are observable. They are things you can see, hear, and feel when you visit a classroom, the kind of things that make a writer feel immediately at home. You know you are in a place created by people who love writing and reading if, for example, you see writing honored and preserved in portfolios or displayed on the wall. The samples probably look a little different from one another because individuality and personal approach are deeply valued by serious writers. Maybe you'll see samples of the teacher's writing displayed, too—a quiet confirmation that he or she is part of this writing community.

You will almost surely find a collection of books, some worn from use, and all readily accessible to students, with a place or places where writers gather to read and share. Maybe you can tell which books are the students' or teacher's favorites because there is a special section for those, or there are written reviews that celebrate what these readers love. The tools of writing are everywhere—pens, pencils, and markers of all types, and varied kinds of paper, from butcher paper to stationery.

Some conditions that foster strong writing are subtle—like the layout of the room. When chairs or desks are arranged for conversation, this gives the message that writing is, at times, a talky process, that writers need to exchange ideas, ask questions, and be mentors for peers. A designated place, say an author's chair, for sharing writing, respects a writer's need for audience. It also says that any writer who reads his or her writing to others deserves a special chair because sharing is an act of courage—as well as a gift to be honored.

A retreat is a must. In one classroom I visited often, the teacher had brought in an old comfy couch she'd picked up at a garage sale, along with a rug, floor pillows, and two lamps. The space she created with these items was incredibly snug, but fully functional because the atmosphere was so welcoming. It was right where we all wanted to be, all the time. And the message about reading was unmistakable.

Writing is also nourished by conversation. When students are working on their writing, conferring, or otherwise sharing, you hear comments that are relevant to the task at hand and respectful of the writer's feelings. Flawless writing is not viewed as a realistic or even a desirable goal. Instead, writers talk about and aim for things like clarity, attention to detail, readability, risk-taking, willingness to try something new, audience sensitivity, an editor's eye, a reviser's ear, and the continual search for voice. There are no absolutes of good and bad. There are only steps forward, and new paths to travel.

A writer's need for talk and interchange is balanced with a need for quiet, reflective time. Time that is not interrupted by announcements, questions, the footsteps of other roaming writers, or even the soft whispers of a corner conference. Such time—which may of necessity be short—is everyone's best chance for total concentration on the writing, and for some writers it is the very lifeline that makes the act of writing possible.

Within this atmosphere, independent writers need to both see and experience writing process. Almost nothing does more to sustain a culture of writing than a teacher who writes with students, thereby underscoring the importance of writing, and also allowing students to see the process—one writer's version of it—as it unfolds. We look at products, samples of writing, all the time in classrooms. And this is an invaluable thing to do because it allows students to examine, think about, and discuss what works and what does not. In addition to reading a play, students need to see a live performance. They need to see what writers do as they put writing together.

How do we do this and still emphasize independence? If students see us modeling process, and then do precisely what we do, isn't that counter to the very independence we want them to achieve? It can be, yes. So we have to be careful. We have to tell them outright, "This is not *the* way to write. This is *one* way." We have to model more than one piece of writing so they can see different versions of our process. We have to model more than one *form* of writing—for instance, a research piece and a poem; a persuasive essay and a memoir. That's because the processes for creating these pieces will—for most writers—vary considerably. We have to talk openly about our preferences—whether we enjoy revision, whether we feel confident editing our own work, whether we like to share what we write. How do these things affect the way we engage in process? Everything we do—from getting ready to wrapping up—may differ from what our student writers do, sometimes dramatically. They need to know that such differences reflect each writer's efforts to find what works best, what is most likely to result in readable writing. Writing workshop is a continual search for one's own best personal process.

For all its flexibility, the core of process remains constant: topic selection, prewriting, drafting, sharing, revising, and editing. Though these steps overlap, though they are recurring, and though they look different in the hands of every writer, they show up in some way, in some form, in each writer's work. This means that when we model process, these fundamental elements must be an integral part of what we share with students. When students understand what is fundamental to process, when they have seen it and tried it themselves, repeatedly, then they are ready to personalize it—and it is then that writing becomes truly powerful.

If your students have seen you struggle to find a topic you liked, or look for a prewriting strategy that would light a fire under you, or stumble, glide, pause, hesitate, scratch your head, and push your way through a draft; if they have helped you revise and seen you *still* not completely satisfied, still trying to figure out why it was not working and what else you could do, then they have gained infinitely more than you could give them with any number of lectures or the best writing process graphic in the world. Perhaps you have even invited a published author into your class to talk about his or her writing process, and talked about how it differed from your own and from that of your students. Now you have a terrific foundation because you are teaching your students that writers *own* their process. They are not subservient to it.

It isn't enough, of course. Your students need to be writers, too. In fact, you want them to be writing all along, even *as you are modeling*. The give-and-take parallels, somewhat, the way we learn to drive. You see someone do it, and then you want to take the wheel for a while. The next time you're the observer, you look for other things, because now you *know* what to look for. You've been there yourself. And when you take the wheel again, you're ready for a whole new level, ready to challenge yourself.

As we learn to write, doing and modeling feed off each other, and each step takes writers closer to independence. Already, your students are beginning to find their own way in, their own strategies. Especially if you are encouraging this. Especially if you are saying things like, "Guess what? Word webs are terrific, but they don't work for everyone. If you need to just plunge in and write, do that. Drafting *is* a kind of prewriting for some people." Or, "Sharing isn't comfortable for everyone. But it can be helpful—particularly if you listen hard for that very comment or response that tells you how your writing is affecting someone else. It may not be something you will always do, but you need to give it a chance." Each person's process is different, but you don't know this until you have experimented with all the pieces and parts that go into creating writing.

The amount of writing students do has enormous bearing on how quickly they will feel ready to take control of their own writing process. In most things we do in life, we start off timidly, and gradually feel the confidence to develop our own style. For a beginning writer, the very fact that process has something we can call identifiable "steps" is a comfort. It gives them a place to begin and end, a way to know when they are "done." The notion that these steps might be recurring or cyclical is confusing to someone who does not write or has not written very much. Writers—by which I mean people who write frequently and for a variety of reasons—discover numerous things about writing just simply by doing it. They learn, for example, that:

- Drafting can go quickly and feel good, or take forever and be agonizing.
- Prewriting or rehearsing sometimes takes longer than drafting.
- Drafting goes better when you know your topic well.
- Writers may go through a recurring cycle of drafting and revising for a long while.
- Revision is not about fixing what is wrong, but about seeing the writing in a new way.
- Revision can be the most satisfying, engaging part of the process.
- Writing does not go from *bad* to *good* but grows, evolves, expands, and reshapes itself just the way thinking grows in the mind.
- Most writing doesn't end up looking at all as the writer thought it would.

- Sharing can make you feel good, but is far more helpful once you learn to read your audience.
- Two people hardly ever agree completely on any piece of writing.
- You can love a piece you've written one day and hate it the next.
- In the end, the writer must decide how and whether to revise.
- In the end, the writer is the most important assessor of his/her own work.
- Good writers are not always good editors, and vice versa.

Writing and more writing and still more writing takes writers to a place of comfort with the process that nothing else can match. No matter how much we know or think we know about writing, there is much that writers must teach themselves, simply by doing it.

How much time should students spend writing each day? An hour would be good. Less is more realistic, but we must recognize it for what it is, a compromise. An hour can make a *significant* difference in both performance and comfort. Writing takes time. Writing takes planning, reflection, collaboration, research, and revision. Teaching writing requires demonstrating, sharing, reading aloud, discussing writing samples, conferring, responding, and more. These things cannot happen quickly. They cannot happen in ten- or fifteen-minute bursts. It is impossible to produce documents of length or depth or significance under the time constraints we place on most of our student writers—and their teachers. When we, as a society, place enough value on the deep thinking that writing requires, we will make time for it.

To gain control of their writing process, students need one more thing: balance. Good writing workshop takes a delicate balance of spontaneity and structure. By *structure* I do not mean application of formulas or rigid rules. I mean consistent expectations about things such as when writing will happen or how much writing time students will have. It may take years to achieve this balance fully. Too often, we wind up structuring things we shouldn't (such as process), thereby suppressing students' thinking, or conversely, leaving some things to chance that work more effectively as part of a routine (such as an established time for writing).

Let's think about routine first, the structured part of writing workshop. I think it helps to write at the same time, or about the same time, each day. I start around 9 a.m. every day, and write before I engage in that greatest of all distractions, email. Between writing times, everything I read or experience, every conversation becomes a well from which I can draw for the drafting I will do tomorrow. As the novelist Henry Miller said, "Most writing is done away from the typewriter, away from the desk. I'd say it occurs in the quiet, silent moments, while you're walking or playing a game, or even talking to someone you're not vitally interested in. You're working, your mind is working, on this problem in the back of your head" (Brodie 1997, 41).

It is good if students know when they will write, on which days, at what time, and for how long. When you anticipate, you observe differently, you think differently, and you remember differently. Your life between writing times is like a walk through the woods during which you are gathering flowers—one here, two there—so that by the time you return home, you can fill the empty vase with a full bouquet.

Students need a way to manage their writing physically. They need folders or portfolios, and a separate place for "keepers" versus those pieces that are still in process or that are simply part of routine practice—focused lessons, for example. *Keepers* are those pieces that seem reflective of a writer's abilities or growth, or that are memorable for any personal reason. Such pieces might be accompanied by a short reflective piece, commentary from the writer on why each piece should be saved.

Unless the student writer or parents have strong feelings about it, I do not advise keeping everything a child writes. For one thing, there is not room for it. We would need trunks, not folders. In addition, it becomes confusing for the writer. When I put together a photo album for our family's trip to the Boundary Waters, I did not include every picture we had taken. I didn't even use one in three. I tried to select those that captured the spirit of the journey, or highlighted the moments we all wanted to hold onto. Students need to review their work in just this way, searching out the pieces that best capture who they are as writers and who they are becoming. We can help, but the choices must be theirs. The very act of selection causes them to look at their work and their personal growth as writers quite differently. Such review, which puts responsibility for self-assessment into the writer's hands, is among the most effective ways of giving students control over their own process.

Students also need consistent guidelines regarding formatting and publishing. Probably in your classroom, no matter what grade you teach, you have books (dictionaries, thesauruses, handbooks, and so on) available for your students, shelved in an easy-to-access place. A collection of handbooks teaches the important lesson that not even professional editors agree on what is correct or preferable, and that's a worthwhile lesson, but it's also confusing for beginning writers.

If you've not already done so, therefore, consider having a specific handbook to which you turn as "the authority" for your classroom—for example, "*Write Source 2000* will be our primary handbook, and this is what I'd like you to consult if you have a question about punctuation or grammar and usage." Heinemann, the publisher of the book you are reading now, favors the *Chicago Manual of Style*, 15th edition, for much of their formatting, including bibliographic entries, and their instructions on this are very clear: "Please do not use APA or MLA bibliographic style in your manuscript. *Chicago* is the standard for our industry, and we have found that its style is the most consistent and efficient" (Heinemann: *Author Guidelines*, 2002, page 28). I like having explicit guidelines like this. It keeps me from having to guess what the editor will favor—and also keeps me from having to redo a bibliography because I followed a nonapproved format. You might not think of bibliographical format as being a controversial issue, but in fact, many matters of style involve preference. So why not make our preferences clear? (It doesn't hurt to acknowledge, of course, that other teachers may take a different stand.)

Some teachers also find it helpful to create a style sheet of the sort publishing houses use. Think of your classroom as your personal publishing house, and let students know your expectations about such things as font size and type, how you'd like titles, headings. or labels to appear, what sort of up-front information (name, date, class period) you want recorded on each paper, margin size, rules about graphics or photos, and so on. Print it up, label it ("Mr. Walker's Classroom Style Sheet"), and pass it out.

Finally, it is important to make assessment consistent. Students should know what we want, what we're hoping for, what we value. They will figure it out anyway, but it's faster, more efficient, and much more fair if we tell them outright. We can do this in a number of ways. First, we should provide students with the criteria we will use to assess their work. Not by just telling them, but by committing the criteria to paper; putting such criteria in print clarifies our own thinking about writing and also says to students, "I believe this so strongly I'm willing to put it on paper so we can refer to it and discuss it—maybe even change it."

Criteria, such as rubrics and checklists, may be the most obvious indicators of what we value in writing—or any performance—but they are not the only indicators. We reinforce what we value by the comments we make aloud or on students' papers, the things we notice within their writing, the things that surprise or delight or annoy us, and the words we use to share what we think or feel. "Great voice!" is a more specific comment than "Great job!" but it is not the same as "I had to read this twice—I couldn't stop laughing over your description of Uncle Bill and the chicken coop." Suppose I do not make *any* comments on the chicken coop paper. In that case, my silence may say to the writer, "Sorry, but voice is not something I respond to particularly." We need to understand the messages we convey by not commenting. We reveal ourselves through our assessments.

We also reveal ourselves and our preferences through what we choose to read aloud—and the way in which we read it. I cannot hope to convince anyone that I care about voice, for instance, if I do not choose selections that resound with voice, if I read in a sort of battle fatigued manner, or if I never laugh aloud or sigh or tear up. When students see us react to the writing of others they gain a sense of the power their own writing may wield. Nothing is so inspiring to a writer as the thought that his or her words may hit someone like a hammer.

Let's say I'm working with students on personal narrative writing or memoir. I want to show them that in such writing, voice is the quality that keeps us reading and that reaches out and touches us, sometimes in more than one way. To describe this, I might choose to read this passage by Garrison Keillor—a moment from his early childhood that captures his Aunt Marie, who had "fat little legs" and worried that no one loved her:

> She sat eating pork roast, mashed potato, creamed asparagus, one Sunday at our house when she said it. We were talking about a trip to the North Shore and suddenly she broke into tears and cried, "You don't care about me. You say you do but you don't. If I died tomorrow, I don't know as you'd even go to my funeral." I was six. I said cheerfully, "I'd come to your funeral," looking at my fat aunt, her blue dress, her string of pearls, her red rouge, the powder on her nose, her mouth full of pork roast, her eyes full of tears. (1987, xix)

This piece is at once funny (because of little Garrison's outburst of loyalty) and simultaneously so deeply sad it reaches right off the page and grabs me by the throat. I can feel Aunt Marie's heart crack, and when I read the piece aloud, students will feel it, too. Then Garrison Keillor will have taught us all a profound lesson about the connection between honest detail and voice. I will know that this part of writing process belongs to students when they are bringing in passages to read to me.

Consistency creates a safe and comfortable environment within which to produce writing. But we must be careful not to structure those parts of writing that need to be spontaneous and free. It would be *dangerously* easy to turn writing process into a lockstep formula. The steps, prewriting/rehearsing, drafting, sharing, revising, editing, and publishing, feel so neat and manageable. Why not prewrite one day, draft the next, revise the following day, and so on? That way, everyone is doing things together, focused lessons match where everyone is in the process, assignments become so much easier, we all publish together, and writing workshop looks very manageable.

When I picture a step-by-step approach, I recall Corinne, a guest at my daughter's eighth birthday party. The children were making masks at large tables. Corinne had finished painting, and was ready to go on to the next step of fixing hair to the top of the mask—only the instructor wanted everyone to work on the same step at the same time. She could see the hair, the very piece she wanted for her mask, but she couldn't reach it, and the instructor refused to hand it to her—yet. It sat there, just beyond her fingertips. Corinne closed her eyes and breathed deeply, tightening her fists. "This project is giving me a headache," she said.

I knew exactly how she felt. Like Corinne, writers work at their own speed and in their own way. They need the freedom to linger or to move ahead. They need the freedom to go back if they need to. When we read, we stop and reflect from time to time on the author's message or intent or voice. We reread passages we did not quite get the first time and rethink the meaning. We skim when the words seem to flow easily, or slow down where the text grows heavy and demanding of our attention. We need to write in the same way and with the same freedom. We cannot write as a team.

Steps within writing process are actually complex processes unto themselves, not really simple steps at all. They not only overlap, but take numerous forms, evolving and adapting to suit a writer's unique style. Independent writers need to know that when we talk about "drafting" or "prewriting" or "rehearsal" or "revision," each of these could include, at some point, any of the following behaviors—or a hundred others:

> reading aloud
> reading silently
> putting copy aside for a time
> sharing the writing with someone else
> taking or ignoring advice
> editing or getting some editing help
> simultaneously creating and crossing out
> turning the ending into the beginning
> starting over, or choosing a new topic altogether
> dreading the reading because the text may sound stupid
> loving the reading because the text is better than you'd remembered
> reading someone else's work (for example, Garrison Keillor's), hoping
> to make your writing sound more like *that*
> writing faster, or slower, seeking the rhythm that works for you
> revising a paragraph that just isn't working, then cutting it totally, and
> then suddenly liking the whole piece better
> taking a walk, using the power of reflection
> pretending you're Stephen King (or any famous writer) and that this is
> all very easy for you
> pretending you're Anne Lamott and so, even if it isn't easy, people will
> love what you write
> turning the music up, or doing what you need to do to shut the world out
> reminding yourself that a rough day is often followed by a productive one

When you really get inside your own writing process, you may discover you do all sorts of things not included in a typical writing process diagram. We all do. And we all feel differently about writing, as the student reflections in Figures 4–1 through 4–6 show.

Individualizing is essential. But how else can we help students take charge of their own writing process? For one thing, we can give them the freedom to leave some drafts unfinished. I mean forever. As a writer, I treasure the right to choose what I will finish and what I will abandon. There is no more reason to finish everything we begin to write than there is to finish everything we begin to read. When it isn't working, there is nothing to be gained from bucking fate. Let go.

Second, we can give our student writers the right to decide what—if anything—will be published. In the world outside the classroom, publishing is a source of personal satisfaction or income or both. Within the classroom, it's a little different. Students have much opportunity to share what they have written informally. They may read pieces aloud from an author's chair or in a response group—or just quietly in a corner to you or to a trusted friend. Some will argue that publication honors students' work, and I agree. But there are other, more quiet ways to honor such work, such as saving it within a portfolio. To some students, writing is extremely personal, and they are uncomfortable having it pulled into the spotlight. We need to honor that, too. Anne Lamott reminds us that publication is not really the point anyway. *Writing* is the point: "Publication is not all that it is cracked up to be. But writing is. It's like discovering that while you thought you needed the tea ceremony for the caffeine, what you really needed was the tea ceremony. The act of writing turns out to be its own reward" (Brodie 1997, 99).

Third, we should encourage student writers to decide for themselves whether their own work is good. I have never had a piece published I did not feel good about on some level, but I have surely written things I felt very good about that I could not get published. In the out-of-classroom world of writing, publishing is a prominent form of assessment. Writers outside school don't get grades or scores (though they may get stars from critics who simply cannot resist reducing everything to numbers). Writers get things published—or not. And when our writing is *not* accepted, we get one of those formal rejection letters. They always seem to be written on very tiny stationery. Maybe publishers don't want to waste paper on rejectees, or perhaps it's their way of saying, "This isn't good news, so why make a big deal of it?"

I saved one such letter just because I was impressed by how politely the publisher managed to say no: "Thank you for sending us your story. While several of us have read it and found it interesting, we feel it is not right for our publishing needs at this time. However, another publisher may feel quite dif-

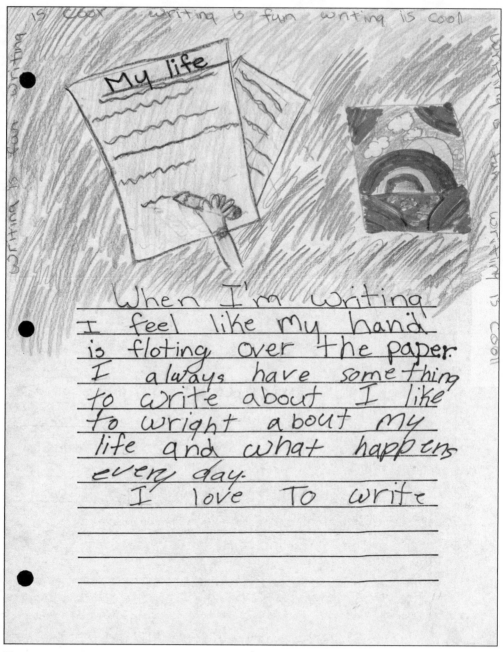

FIGURE 4-1

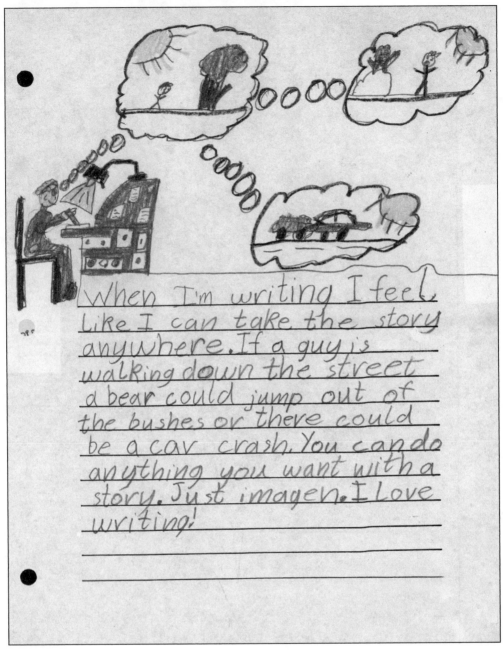

When I'm writing I feel
like I can take the story
anywhere. If a guy is
walking down the street
a bear could jump out of
the bushes or there could
be a car crash. You can do
anything you want with a
story. Just imagen. I Love
writing!

FIGURE 4–2

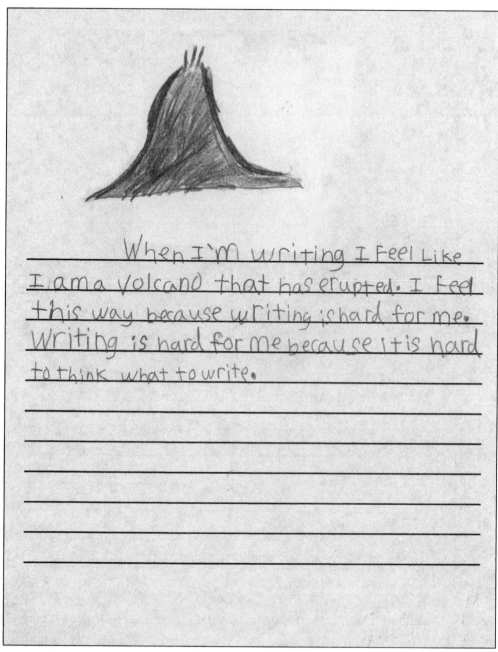

When I'M writing I feel Like I am a volcano that has erupted. I feel this way because writing is hard for me. Writing is hard for me because it is hard to think what to write.

FIGURE 4–3

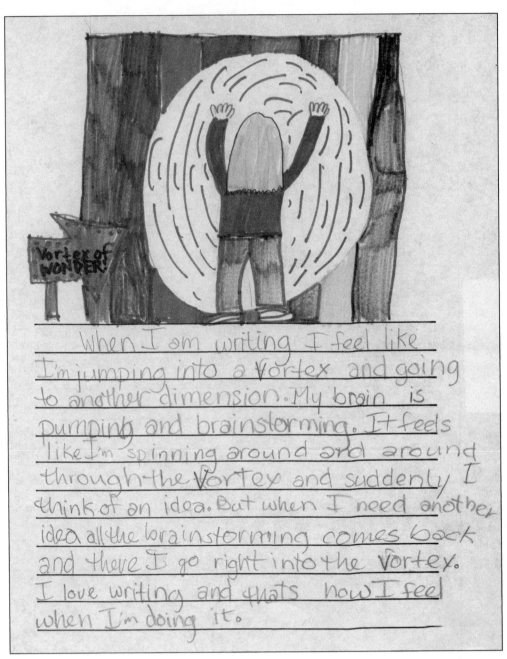

When I am writing I feel like I'm jumping into a Vortex and going to another dimension. My brain is pumping and brainstorming. It feels like I'm spinning around and around through the Vortex and suddenly I think of an idea. But when I need another idea all the brainstorming comes back and there I go right into the Vortex. I love writing and thats how I feel when I'm doing it.

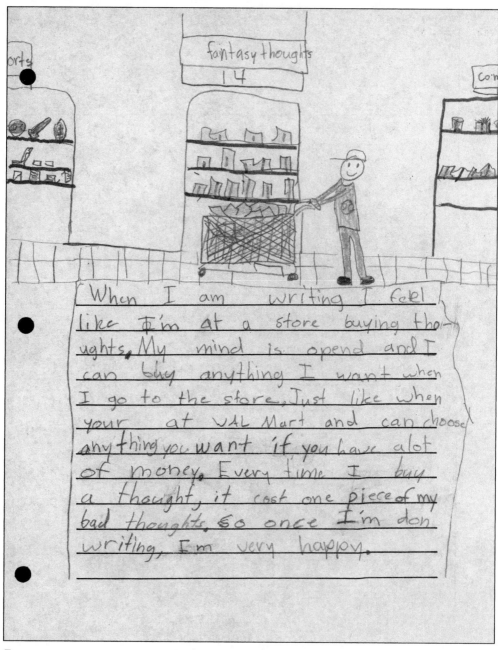

fantasy thoughts
14

When I am writing I feel like I'm at a store buying thoughts. My mind is opend and I can buy anything I want when I go to the store. Just like when your at WAL Mart and can choose anything you want if you have alot of money. Every time I buy a thought, it cost one piece of my bad thoughts. So once I'm don writing, I'm very happy.

FIGURE 4–5

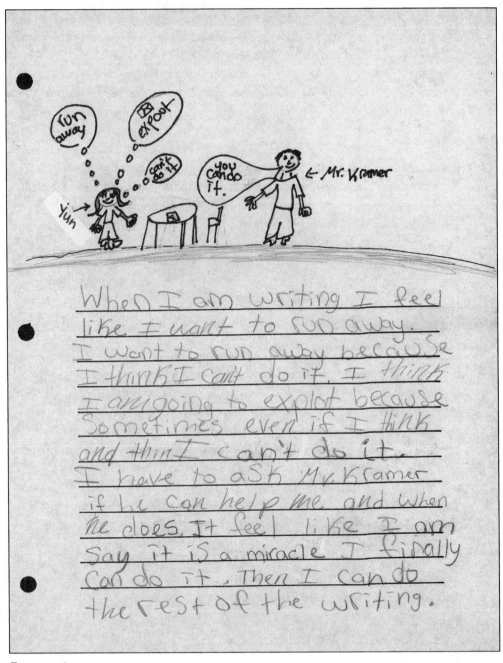

FIGURE 4–6

ferently, so we prefer not to offer more specific comments." It's courteous enough, I suppose, but simultaneously annoying because it dances around the heart of the matter: the reason behind the rejection. We can't do that with our students. We can't say, "Your paper was interesting, but it just doesn't meet my curricular needs at this time." We need to explain ourselves.

Rejections are sometimes quite appropriate, of course. I'm honestly happy, at this point, that a lot of the pieces I originally wanted published never made it. But rejection does not always mean a piece isn't good. That's the thing. That's the reason writers need to keep believing. Believing in themselves, believing in their own process, believing in the work that comes from it. Consider this opportunity missed, for example: "It is impossible to sell animal stories in the U.S.A." (Brodie 1997, 95). This was one publisher's response to George Orwell's *Animal Farm*.

So, short of appearing on the *New York Times'* bestseller list or winning the Newberry, how do writers decide if their work is good? I have one very simple rule: *Did I keep it?* If I kept it, if I return to it and read it now and then, if I like it as much five years after writing it as I did the day I finished revising, then I know it's good. I want students to know—*really* know—about their own writing in this way. True freedom within writing process means freedom from the limitations of outside assessment. That's not to say that we close our ears to critics—good critics and good editors (some of the best readers among us) have insights we would be foolish to ignore. But we don't want students' perceptions of their writing to be bound solely by our judgments or grades or scores. Especially when we know how fallible we are. Especially when we know how tired or distracted we are sometimes when we read their work. We want them to have faith in their own personal assessment: *I kept it. It's good.*

Finally, we should listen to our students, allowing them to be coaches and mentors for us. We must let them share what they know—with one another and with us (see the following advice). For as all writers and travelers know, the reward for surviving the journey is having stories to tell.

Advice from Fourth Grade Writers

- If you're writing about yourself, my advice is to always tell the truth.
- Be true to yourself and other people.
- My advice for a beginner is start with fiction because if you do nonfiction, you have to do lots and lots of research.

(continued)

- You have to indent to start a paragraph. That is what writing is all about.
- Write a lot.
- Write a good story someone like you would like to read.
- The first advice is to indent—and then think where you can put a dot.
- When you are stumped, ask a neighbor for ideas.
- The advice I have about writing is never give up.
- Make it as interesting as it can be.
- Make sense and spell right.
- Don't talk to people. It distracts you.
- Make it fun or you will never love it like me.
- Be yourself. Don't try to copy some famous writer.
- Be happy with what you do.
- Never stop writing.
- Put all you've got into it. Then your book will be talked about!
- My only advice is to love writing with all your heart.
- Even if it's boring, stick with it. Don't give up until you're done.
- Don't copy other people's writing.
- Get a good grip on your pencil. Then, make it interesting.

Advice from High School Writers

- Make an outline of your ideas before you start writing.
- Avoid using the word "you."
- Use powerful verbs to give your paper voice.
- Write about things you enjoy; writing about the little things can make for great writing.
- Turn off the critic in your head.
- I try not to think while I'm actually writing. I type/write all of the thoughts coming into my head and only after I've completed those ideas do I go back and make sense of the ideas I plotted. It makes my writing pure and uncensored. Otherwise

the human mind tends to doubt its thoughts and leave out the points worth making.

- Always know what you want to accomplish before writing.
- Know the main thing you want to say. Write it down and paste it to the top of your computer.
- It's never good to jump around. Always try to stay focused and organized.
- If an unrelated thought pops into your head, don't reject it too fast. Give it a chance. Maybe it is related, like a distant cousin.
- Write what you feel. Honesty and personality can spark great writing.
- When I'm pushing for a deadline, I clear my brain of all interior/exterior distractions, and let loose on the keyboard, emptying all good ideas in my mind into the computer. Usually, once I get one good solid idea, it just flows from my brain to my hands to a finished document.
- Find a place to write where you feel comfortable.
- Write from the heart. From what you feel, from what you remember.
- Brainstorm, get your topic in mind, sit down and start writing.
- Don't go to the fridge. Keep writing.
- Make sure what you're writing keeps your attention. If not, it's not going to keep the reader's.
- Cut the b.s., and don't state the obvious.
- Don't be afraid to break the rules.

The Real Scoop: A Writer Talks About His Writing Process

SNEED B. COLLARD

I am enormously impressed by teachers who teach the writing process to young people. For me, and for most professional writers, writing is a subconscious activity, one we instinctively pursue with only vague definition. Yet, I love to pass on any insights I've gained to student writers in the classrooms I frequently visit. Here are a few things I share with them.

To begin, let's assume that I've gone through the process of choosing a general topic (usually topics *find me* as I'm exploring the natural world—it's always something about which I am curious). My next step—and I believe this is true of most writers—is to do *all* the research I can think of at the time. This is essential because without sufficient knowledge sitting in my brain and at my feet, I don't really know what I'm going to write about—no matter what I've told my editors beforehand. I need every bit of information I can gather to organize my book or even know what kind of approach I'll take.

For me, real world research is a big part of prewriting, and it might take me from the Great Barrier Reef to the plains of Iowa or anywhere in between. It means taking a close look at the world through my own eyes, then talking with other scientists and investigators, anyone whose observational skills I can combine with my own to build a larger or more precise version of reality. It also means taking endless notes and collecting endless piles of scientific papers or other literature. The thing is, though, that big pile of research will be whittled way, *way* down through the process of writing. A draft is never an inflated version of your research; it's a tiny fragment of what's best or most interesting.

Once the research is done, I can give my subject more shape and focus. Keeping in mind the length of the book I want to write, I sift through the material for:

1. topics that are high-interest (Why include boring ones?)
2. topics that hang together: those related enough to fit together logically without introducing a vast new subject
3. topics that tell stories

This last point is vital. The older I get, the more I realize how much people love stories, whether in fiction or my own specialty, nonfiction. For almost anyone, reading a story is more riveting than scanning facts. Storytelling also lends itself to better writing. It demands more active verbs, better description, and more logical organization. It's no surprise that some of my most successful titles, including *The Forest in the Clouds*, *The Deep-Sea Floor*, and *A Platypus, Probably*, are basically nonfiction stories.

Once I have the general scope of the emerging story in my head, I organize details in a way that makes sense, paying special attention to what a reader needs to know *first*, and using that as a stepping stone to more complex information. Then I sketch out an organizational structure and plunge in.

Contrary to the way many people envision writing process, I do not bulldoze my way through a rough draft and then revise. Personally, I *can't stand* for my sentences and paragraphs not to flow easily from one to another. If I write a sentence and I know it doesn't work, I make myself get at least a palatable version down before I continue. If a paragraph doesn't follow well from the one before it, I'll either cut it and start over, or go back and change the preceding paragraph.

That doesn't mean I demand perfection at each step. I just means I don't want to trip and fall on my face, even during the early stages. As a result, what I call my "first draft" is usually, in reality, my eighth or tenth. Once that draft is complete, the real polishing—and fun—begins.

I *love* tweaking a manuscript. It feels good to find sentences, paragraphs, or even whole sections I can cut to make the piece stronger or clearer. If any portion does not contribute, it needs to go. It's convenient to revise by looking for literary flab since most first drafts are much too long. With each slash, the manuscript gets leaner, cleaner, and more readable.

I've learned that organization is not something you can wholly plan ahead of time. Often, I am not sure how information should be organized until after the first draft is complete. My book *The Prairie Builders*, for example, was originally supposed to focus on the reintroduction of an endangered butterfly called the Regal Fritillary into a new tallgrass prairie project in Iowa. While visiting Iowa to do research for this book, I discovered that the prairie project itself was actually the main story. Still, when I wrote the first draft, I tried to force the butterfly story into the lead. It wasn't working.

After struggling through the manuscript several times, I finally realized—with an editor's help—that I needed to begin with the prairie and work in the butterfly story later. I swapped things around, wrote a new beginning, and just like *that*, the manuscript came together. As writers, we get so hung up on seeing a manuscript in a certain way that sometimes it takes a new perspective to spot the underlying organizational flow.

And this brings me to another point about editing—or revising. It is *invaluable* to have others read my work. I am fortunate to belong to a writer's group full of accomplished, diverse writers. We meet once a month to read each other's work aloud. The results are astonishing. By listening to another person read my words, I catch things I would never notice reading my work silently to myself. Moreover, I've learned that each person in the group hears things a little differently. All these perspectives go together to give me a true picture of what needs improvement. Group collaboration is something I encourage for all writers, both professionals and students.

SNEED B. COLLARD III *graduated with honors in marine biology and specializes in nonfiction for young readers of all ages. A prolific writer with a passion for research, he has published more than thirty award-winning books for children, including* The Prairie Builders, Beaks!, The Forest in the Clouds, *and* The Deep-Sea Floor; *2005 will see at least eight new titles published, including his first novel,* Dog Sense, *from Peachtree Publishers and the literary nonfiction picture book* Platypus, Probably *from Charlesbridge. He is known for his ability to weave drama into literally any research-based writing. Currently, Sneed lives in Missoula, Montana, with his wife, Amy, and son, Braden.*

Five
The Right to Write Badly

Somewhere along the way, school became a place where it is not all right to fail—ever. What a shame. Fear of failure increases stress and minimizes willingness to take chances. Without risk, it is nearly impossible to grow as a writer.

Non-risk-takers can rise to a level of competence, to be sure. They can write business letters and emails and complete reports that contain the necessary data. Is that enough? Is that all we want for our students? When they could do so much more? Just think. They could write an essay that's read on NPR—or the speech that might swing voters in a candidate's favor. They could write a letter someone would save forever, a poem that would win a lover's heart, a comic essay that would lift a person out of depression, a story that would become a child's favorite, an argument that would make a legislator vote differently, a textbook from which someone would learn things she would recall years later. It is unlikely to happen, though, if we insist that they write well or even adequately *all the time*. No one does this. No one who writes to be read, anyway. As Stephen King says, "Only God gets it right the first time" (2000, 212).

A person weaving through a maze makes wrong turns, but uses that experience to figure out the path. A doctor uses every diagnosis, right and wrong, to refine her skills. When a child takes his first tentative steps and falls, we applaud the walking and cheer for him when he gets up. We never say, "Well, he's no walker, that's for sure." We know—we *believe*—that he will not only walk, but run, climb mountains, ski the steepest slopes, dance the tango. Falling down is

You have to allow yourself the liberty of writing poorly. You have to get the bulk of it done, and then you start to refine it. You have to put down less than marvelous material just to keep going to whatever you think the end is going to be—which may be something else altogether by the time you get there.

—LARRY GELBART
Writing Changes Everything
ed. Deborah Brodie

nothing. That's how the tango looks early on. Too bad we're not as quick to recognize early writing success. Not only would we be more tolerant of experimentation, but we would encourage risk instead of fearing that it would only lead to further, more dramatic, failure. And ironically, we would set the bar for eventual achievement much, much higher.

To understand the power of a long-distance perspective, watch a good coach. My daughter, Nikki, learned to swim when she was about four. Like many children, she knew she could not swim. Fortunately for her, she had a teacher who disagreed—a teacher who saw *swimmer* written all over Nikki as she stood on the cold tile with her bare feet, clutching the swimming goggles she didn't even know how to put on.

On the first lesson, Rick asked Nikki to get into the pool. That's it. No strokes—no kicking—no floating even. She only had to get in. "Good for you—you're on your way," he told her. Next lesson: "Put your face in the water." This seems like nothing at all to a swimmer, but to a nonswimmer, it's a big step. Rick came through: "That's the toughest part, and you did it," he told her. "Everything gets easier after this."

For a while, that was true. Nikki learned to blow bubbles, kick from the edge, and even make her way across the shallow end of the pool holding onto a kickboard. What she could not seem to do was to float on her own, no supports. Rick encouraged her endlessly: "It's shallow. You can stand if you need to. I'll watch you. I'll *catch* you. You can do it. You are already doing it with the board. All you're doing is letting go, letting the board float on its own. . . ." She hung on the edge, upright, as if determined to prove him wrong.

This is the moment at which, if we were to assess Nikki—take a snapshot and evaluate it (most assessments are snapshots)—we'd have to say, "Well, nonswimmer. She's in the water, and that's worth a point, but she's not moving."

Rick was a master teacher, though. He had two qualities I love in a teacher. In place of failure, he saw future success. Instead of the frightened child who clung to the edge of the pool, he saw the swimmer she would be. And he was always willing to try another approach. "Nikki," he said one day, "just float to me. You don't have to actually *swim*. Just push off with your feet and float over to me." I held my breath as she bent her knees and gave a shove—then floated three feet. She popped up with a huge grin beneath her goggles. She had tasted success and found it delicious. Rick backed up so she could go five feet, then ten. And after that—we couldn't get her out of the water.

"You did it!" I told him.

He shook his head. "She did it. I just believed."

I sometimes wonder how many of our nonwriters could float if we, like Rick, just changed the language a little bit. If we said, "Don't worry about creating a piece of writing—just write me a note about what happened."

When I sit down at my keyboard, I don't want to feel the pressure of needing to create something masterful and moving. Like all writers, I would love for that to happen, of course, but I know that most days I will write a lot of words I'll end up simply throwing away. That's the way writing works. You need to create a lot of garbage to get at the heart of it—the real message, the thing you want most to say, the voice that is really you. The book I finished last year, *Creating Writers*, fourth edition, wound up at four hundred pages. Had I kept everything I wrote in producing that book, it would have been well over two thousand pages. Luckily for my readers, I didn't. It's rare for me to keep more than a fourth of what I write (and many writers keep far less). So knowing this, how can we ask students to consistently produce strong, clear, coherent text with a first or second effort? How unreasonable is that?

In order to understand the need to create schlock, we have to look at how writing works. We have to be writers ourselves. Nonwriters often imagine that writers focus on a topic (*cats*), think up what they will say *(Cats are clever enough to live in the wild without the aid of humans)*, and then write it down. So the process goes like this: identify the topic, think through the topic, write the piece. This is why nonwriters also think of revision chiefly as editing. After all, what else is left to do? Actually, writing is much like spinning a web:

> A spider starts an orb web by floating out a silk line and waiting for it to touch down on some object. Then with dry, unstretchy silk, it spins a sturdy frame and a temporary spiral. When the spider goes back to put in the sticky trap lines, it moves from spoke to spoke, biting off the dry lines, recycling the old silk by eating it, and tapping down the new sticky silk to fasten it securely. A spider works an hour or more to make a web and may use as much as 200 feet of silk. (Facklam 2001, 6)

That first silk line is like a writer's first thought. It may exist in the form of a big concept (*feral cats*) or a first line. Some writers begin with the first line in their heads, like the opening line of a play. Then, if all goes well, that first line is strong enough to become the foundation for other thoughts. Like the spider connecting silk strands, the writer connects ideas, "biting off the dry lines," and strengthening the rest so that it forms a pattern, a spiral, of which every strand is an integral part.

Like web building, writing can be a lonely business. In the beginning, it's just you, spinning silk, sending out that first strand and hoping it will stick. I might begin with a line like this:

> Feral cats are those clever enough to live independently, with little or no support from humans.

That's a beginning of sorts, but where is it going to take me? Want to try something interesting? Write down my line about feral cats right now. Put this book down and try writing from that line for just five minutes, and see where it takes *you*. Then come back.

Did you do it? OK, here's the point: You went one direction with that line, but I will go another. Compare the two, and you see how fragile the "hold" of that initial line is. It's probably not strong enough to support the final piece. We know this instinctively, and so we wander, you and I, in search of a real thesis, and we wind up in completely different places. Further, because we're searching, the writing is likely to sound random, maybe a little disjointed. And no wonder, for we are creating not just physical text, but the thinking behind it. We need to write in this disjointed way at first so we can create some material—some silk—out of which to spin something stronger later on.

I know a little about feral cats because we have so many here in rural Oregon. So, here's where my thinking takes me, first draft:

> Feral cats are those clever enough to live independently, with little or no support from humans. They begin their lives, usually, because they've been abandoned by humans, though some are born in the wild, and feral cats are prolific breeders. Nature is not always kind to cats, however, and many of the young do not survive. Those who do are relentless, fierce hunters, and in areas where feral cats are numerous, many native species may be wiped out altogether. Though the feral cat is not a large predator, it will take on fairly large birds, such as a quail, as well as literally any species of mouse, rat, or gopher, and smaller rabbits. Some hunt snakes and lizards. Feral cats themselves are prey to many hunters, including hawks, eagles, and coyotes. Further, many succumb to disease, including rabies. In fact, feral cats may be the single biggest carriers of rabies. And of course, many starve to death or fall victim to harsh weather. Because feral cats have a history of being domesticated, they do not fear humans, and for this reason can be dangerous. People who enjoy the romantic notion of a small cat as a hunter may feed feral cats, or even have them vaccinated if they will tolerate being handled. Is this a kindness or does it just make a bad situation worse?

It is hard to look at your own writing with the same objectivity you'd apply to someone else's work, but let me give it a shot. I see a functional, if not passionate lead, and numerous related ideas, some of which need to be expanded. My sentences are varied, but rhythmically jarring. The organization feels jumpy—

here's a thought, and here's a thought, and here's a thought, as if I'm pushing a cart through a market and grabbing whatever appeals to me on the spot.

If this were someone else's writing, I might think as I read it, "Well, this writer can shape a sentence, but she doesn't have much sense of the whole. I wouldn't want to read fifty pages of this." If I read this piece aloud, which I always do with my writing, I would revise it significantly. I'd reorder details, and condense. Here are the first few lines, as my ear tells me to revise them:

> Feral cats are those clever enough to live independently, with little or no support from humans. Most have been abandoned by their owners, though some are born in the wild. Feral cats are prolific breeders, but as a result of harsh weather, starvation, disease—notably rabies—and predators, only a handful survive. Those who do are relentless, fierce hunters. Despite their relatively small size, they will take on fairly large birds, such as quail, as well as snakes, lizards, and literally any species of mouse, rat, gopher, or rabbit. In areas where feral cats are numerous, many native species may be wiped out.

Better, I think. Smoother. It reminds me of Cary Grant's assessment of Grace Kelly in an early scene from the Hitchcock film *To Catch a Thief:* "Quietly attractive." In a similar assessment spirit, this piece might be dubbed "pleasantly readable." I can smooth out and pretty up sentences all I want, but without a single strand of silk to catch hold, I haven't gotten around to putting in much substance. I have no central message, no line from which every detail will radiate to form a pattern the reader can follow. Let's try again:

> Next time you let your cat out, and wonder where he's headed, you might also ask yourself what the odds are that he'll even come back. Not all do. Feral cats—domestic cats gone wild—are those clever enough to live independently, with little or no support from humans. Most have been abandoned by their owners or have simply gone beyond the backyard to seek their fortune elsewhere, and increasing numbers are born in the wild. Feral cats are prolific breeders, but as a result of harsh weather, starvation, disease—notably rabies—and predators, only a handful of kittens survive. Yet, against all odds, their numbers are growing. For one thing, humans who romanticize the notion of cats returning to the wild often feed them, or even vaccinate them, if the cats will allow it. For another, feral cats who make it on their own for more than a month or two are relentless, fierce hunters. After all, they have no choice. Despite their relatively small size, they will take on fairly large birds like quail, as well as

snakes, lizards, and literally any species of mouse, rat, gopher, or rabbit. The offspring of these skilled hunters tend to inherit their parents' talents. So much so, in fact, that in areas where feral cats are numerous, many native species may be wiped out. This pushes humans toward a difficult but unavoidable decision: Should feral cats be hunted as a way of protecting the environment—or left alone, despite the havoc they wreak in ecological circles across the country?

The last line, a question, feels secure to me. It's the foundational line for my web: whether feral cats should be hunted or left on their own. Notice it comes at the end of the piece, not the beginning. We have conditioned ourselves and sometimes conditioned our students to think that a topic sentence or thesis sentence should come at the beginning of a piece. Often, it falls more naturally at the end because writing is thinking, and we work *toward* meaning.

Notice that it took me three drafts just to get to an opening enticing enough to lure readers in, and a thesis strong enough to support any real expansion. It isn't "whole" yet; I've danced around the topic without taking a position and without getting into the arguments for either side. But it does hang together. The connections that first existed just in my head are now on paper so the reader doesn't have to build them. I have "bitten off" some unneeded lines, and the piece as a whole now has a perceptible shape—which makes it much easier to follow. Also, I've generated enough copy that I can begin to think about form. Though it's evolving into a persuasive essay, I could, if I wanted, turn this into a poem—written from the cat's point of view, perhaps.

In school, writers seldom create more than two drafts. We may call the second draft a "final," but this is a misnomer, one that leads to a misguided sense of how real-world revision works. It is almost impossible, unless you get very, *very* lucky, unless your topic has been living in your head for a long, long while, to go from first thinking to working draft in just two tries. A writer may rework a draft for publication three or four times, put it away for a while, and then rework it three or four more. Sometimes, this process goes through several cycles, each of them a combination of rehearsing, drafting, and revision. There is not time for this in school, not with every draft anyway, but we could do this: first, come clean with students about how extended true revision really is, so that they know what they are doing is usually an approximation of such revision; and second, encourage extensive revision on at least *one* draft produced during the year so that they could see and feel the difference. Then they could know that first drafting is really first thinking, throwing out a silk line and hoping it will catch.

Face it. Not all students live for revision. Some will say of a first draft, "I'm happy with my writing just the way it is. I don't want to change a thing." This usually means they are not reading like writers or have difficulty gaining any distance from their work because they have not left it alone long enough. Maybe they just don't want to revise, regardless of how good, or problematic, the writing is. Revision doesn't interest them much because it's always been done at the behest of someone else and it's never been all that much fun. Or, maybe—let's be optimistic—it actually *is* pretty good. That happens. Now and again, a writer creates something he or she is quite happy with right out of the box, much the way a batter one day steps to the plate and hits the ball out of the park on the first swing. But that is rare. So when a student says, "I'm happy," we need to respond, without irony but with sincere anticipation, "Tell me what you feel especially good about. What really worked for you in this piece?" Usually we, and they, discover that the thinking is still in process after all. Or, on the other hand, we may learn about some strengths we overlooked at first glance.

Almost always, writers need time to explore the landscape, capturing the flow of ideas in search of their own thinking. If we trust the power of thinking, we will give our student writers the freedom to explore, to write badly in order to work their way through to the point where they are writing well. How do we give them the self-confidence needed to do this?

For one thing, we need to write more and assess less. When everything (or almost everything) students write is assessed, they learn to be careful. They write to please the assessor. They keep their writing short so there will be less to assess and write in generalities so no one will take offense. They use words they can spell and avoid punctuation that they feel unsure of. They minimize voice in order to sound "objective." They choose topics they think others will approve of. In short, they do the very things that make strong writing performance all but impossible.

Moreover, it is stressful to be assessed continually. It can feel as if the Great Assessor is following us about with a Clipboard and the Royal Checklist. Further, maybe we're not piling up all the check marks we could—or should. Then, instead of tackling problems, as all writers need to do, our instinct is to hide them.

In her brilliant memoir *My Thirteenth Winter*, writer and poet Samantha Abeel talks of her struggles with numbers, and the extraordinary effort it took to hide her difficulties: "Despite my struggles, elementary school had become a completely familiar environment. There, I had been able to successfully string together webs of coping and compensation strategies that allowed me to mask what I could not do or did not know" (2003, 44). Sam, a verbally adept and gifted writer, had difficulty making change, telling time, or working the combination on a lock, and feared that if the truth were revealed, her teachers and classmates would no longer see her as intelligent and capable:

I believed that if anyone found out what I couldn't do or how hard basic things like opening my locker were for me, they would feel like I had been lying to them—they would wonder why I hadn't said anything up to now. They would think that I didn't belong. They would see the smart, wise, well-behaved, talented Sam for who she really was—a terrified, lost, inept girl. (49)

We are Sam. We wear masks of success, all of us. We fear—teachers and student writers alike—that someone will find out the truth: that we are not always perfect, that we make mistakes, that not every performance is a success. Most of us just aren't as brave as Sam. We don't feel comfortable admitting our fear. We feel that as long as we can perform on the assessment, we can keep up the charade because a test score or a GPA can define us. The truth is, we are already successful, more so than we realize, just by virtue of making the effort. We are not defined by an individual performance or by the test score stamped upon it. We are defined, as Sam makes clear, by the struggle itself:

> Over the years I have also come to view my learning disability as a rather strange and unusual gift. I believe it has allowed me to develop strengths I might not have otherwise developed. I spent so many years as a young child honing my observation skills, learning to read the small facial gestures of people, and studying their changing moods, reactions, and patterns of behavior. I needed these skills to survive. However, now this same ability is an asset as I try to reach out and help others who are struggling. (2003, 201)

Just because we do not assess everything, at least not formally, is no sign we should not be *writing*, however. We do not write so that we can be assessed. We write in order to learn how. Donald Graves, one of our most respected teachers of writing, says that he writes every day, following the philosophy traditionally attributed to Pliny the Elder: *No day without a line.* We should encourage our students to write each day also. It keeps them in writing shape. All the strategies, all the encouragement, all the positive thinking in the world will be of little avail if students do not develop a basic comfort with writing—with just doing it.

In addition, we need realistic goals. Luckily for us, Pliny did not say, "Never a day without a masterpiece." But sometimes we act as if he did. If we take away a writer's right to ever write badly, if we say, "Hold on, here—let's make each piece you create at least respectable," we do just the opposite of what we intend. We slow the writer's progress. We don't have enough time to insist on bravura performances. We need to get out of our writers' way while they get comfortable facing down the blank page. Then we can bring in some strategies and work on style. Comfort *first*.

Daily writing is routine for most professional writers, who often feel their work suffers from breaks. Stephen King claims to write ten pages, or the equivalent of about two thousand words a day (2000, 154). Doing so, he claims, creates an energy that keeps the work fresh:

> If I don't write every day, the characters begin to stale off in my mind—they begin to seem like characters instead of real people. The tale's narrative cutting edge starts to rust and I begin to lose my hold on the story's plot and pace. Worst of all, the excitement of spinning something new begins to fade. The work starts to feel like work, and for most writers that is the smooch of death. (153).

In many classrooms, writing is an event: *Time for writing!* The more we adopt this approach, the more unnatural we make writing feel—and the more pressure we put on students to make every writing act a performance to remember. By contrast, very little fanfare accompanies reading in most classrooms (apart from direct reading instruction). Students read all the time, from textbooks, notes on the chalkboard or overhead, teacher instructions, trade books, their own notes, and the writing of others. Reading doesn't have quite the ready-set-go feeling of writing, where we prepare, then commit the act, then reflect on what we've just done, as if it were so unusual that we have to review it just to get perspective on the whole event. Our students will be stronger, better writers when it feels as natural to write in school as it feels to read, and when it is as integral to learning in all subjects.

Writing across the curriculum is one clear way to provide extended opportunities for writing, and thereby increase students' comfort level. Unfortunately, such writing is so closely connected with research that we forget to explore other possibilities. Not that research writing isn't critical. It takes students beyond self to the world of information. It turns the writer into a teacher, and with that goes the responsibility to be clear, focused, thorough, and audience-sensitive. This is some of the most important writing our students do.

In addition, students can use writing in all subjects to record thoughts and questions, to document their learning process: *How did you figure out the square root of 6561? How did you know where the trains would meet? How is gross domestic product calculated? What do you predict world geography might look like one million years from now? What is the likelihood scientists can accurately predict earthquakes twenty years from now? What are some strategies for improving spelling skills?* Writing of this type is not usually (and should not be) assessed, but it needs to happen because it helps students use language to think clearly. We assume we know what is going on inside our own heads until we are challenged to put it on paper. That simple act brings us face to face with the fuzziness in our own thinking, the blank spaces and looming holes, the missing connections. How many times have you said about a topic, "Oh, I know that. I get that. I understand." And yet, if you were asked to write a summary—of how a computer works, how hurricanes are formed, how federal interest rates affect borrowing, or how the heart functions—you might struggle. Perhaps you would wonder what the main point was after all. You would search for words to explain what it is exactly that you "get." You would fumble for a way to begin—or end. You only need one experience like this to know how important it is for students to document their thinking—and use that thinking to stretch. When we read, we take in information. When we write, we refine it. Reading is like shopping for groceries. Writing requires us to bring things home, order them, put them on the shelves. Where's the peanut butter? The reader says, "Oh it's here somewhere—I remember seeing it." The writer says, "It's right here—I put it on the second shelf next to the grape jelly."

Confidence also comes from seeing yourself grow as a writer, but this can be difficult to do. Can you say how your own writing has changed in the past five years, or ten, or twenty? How much of the writing you created from kindergarten through high school did you save? I am extremely sorry to say that I do not have a shred of mine. We need to encourage writers to hold onto their writing, and to think about just how they can best do that. The writing folder is a writer's friend. Like a well-kept album, it captures snapshots of writing in various stages of writing process.

A writing folder is also a good place to keep pieces from which the writer has learned something important. Once a writer begins saving things routinely, dating them, and recording what he or she is learning, a writing folder may evolve into a portfolio, and when this happens, the writer gets the boost of energy that comes from seeing that he or she is getting somewhere after all. Watching your own writing skill evolve is like watching a plant grow. It happens so slowly you have almost no sense of it without occasional snapshots you can later lay out and say, "Look at that! Look how different it was just a few weeks ago."

Our goal as teachers should not be to fill the world with perfect text, or even acceptable text. Our goal should be to take students to such a place of comfort with writing that they will persist through three pages of random thought to an emerging clarity on page four because they have not one shred of doubt they will get there. After all, only nonwriters fear failure. Writers know clutter and roadblocks and random thinking are all part of the process.

From comfort comes many good things. The comfortable diver goes off the high board one day and everyone cheers. The next day, she does it backward, then puts in a triple somersault and a double spin. "Where does that courage come from?" we ask. From comfort comes willingness to risk, and from risk, Anne Lamott assures us, comes writing that matters: "If something inside you is real, we will probably find it interesting, and it will probably be universal. So you must risk placing real emotion at the center of your work. Write straight into the emotional center of things. Write toward vulnerability." (1995, 226)

In 1987, an eighth-grade student writer took such a risk during the Oregon State Writing Assessment. With very little time on his side, he took us into his emotional center with the story of a 4-H calf he had raised. The calf's name was Ginweed, and it was a name I would never forget. Jason's story grabbed me by the throat the very first time I read it, and never let go. Each time I shared it aloud with a group of teachers, the intensity of their response was palpable. I had to choke back the tears on the last line. I still do. Jason's paper did not have perfect spelling; the original copy had almost *no punctuation at all*; but if the piece is read in a way that reflects the writer's natural sense of rhythm—which wasn't hard to capture in this piece—listeners cannot hear those things. What Jason's story had, and what everyone heard, was *voice*. The voice of a gifted storyteller who could have turned in a safe performance—four or five correct lines—but who dared, despite challenges of spelling and punctuation, to be a writer. Here is an edited version of the story that moves me as much today as it did with that first memorable reading, years ago.

"Ginweed"

Jason Kelleher

It was an early summer morning when Mom woke me up and said, "Go set the barn up for milking." I tried to pretend that I didn't hear her, but it didn't work. Next thing I knew she was running at me with a glass of water and a pancake turner, swinging it in the air like a baseball bat. It didn't take long for me to get out of that bed and grab my pants—but then she threw the water all over me and my clothes. Then she grabbed me and my clothes and threw both of us outside.

After I got them on, I started to walk down to the barn. Jerry, my older brother, was haying cows. I went to check Ginger, our Jersey cow. She was ready to calve. But when the rest of the cows saw me, they tried to run and splattered cow manure all over me. When I got to the barn, I saw Ginger lying in her pen with a wet cold ball of fur. Ginger had died while calving, but her calf was all right. Ginger was Mom's cow, so when she died it shook my mom up plenty. Mom came up with the name "Ginweed" from the G in Ginger's name. So Mom called the calf Ginweed.

Ginweed didn't look very good most of the time. Mom thought for sure she was going to die because she wouldn't eat. But luckily for some reason she made it through the summer's heat and winter's coldness and breezes. I was always looking for a good show calf, and for some reason I knew inside myself this was the calf for me. She finally was old enough to show in the county fair. The date for the fair was August first, and it was now July 15.

My birthday was July 20 and I'd be twelve. So in those five days I tried to let Mom know I needed a show halter without making it sound as if I knew what I was getting for my gift.

On July 18, I took Ginweed out and practiced walking her around. She wasn't too cooperative, and sometimes she got downright mean. That made me kinda mad, so next time she hit me with her head, I doubled up my fist and hit her back, but I think it hurt me more than it did her.

July 20 finally came, and Mom let me sleep in till nine o'clock. She said that was the least she could do because she couldn't afford anything else. But I knew she was kidding—at least I hoped she was. After dinner, Ma brought out a cake with twelve candles on it while everyone sang "Happy Birthday." I wished I would get my halter for Ginweed. But then I could only blow out ten candles, so I thought for sure I wasn't gonna get what I wanted. About that time Dad came out and in his hand he had a black leather halter and chrome-colored chain.

After I was done with dinner I went out to Ginweed's stall and showed her the halter. In the other hand I had some cake. I think she was more interested in that, so I took it and mixed it with some grain and gave it to her. Then I went in and went to sleep.

July 27 was finally here, and I'd just gotten done washing and brushing Ginweed with my sister's brush and Mom's dish soap. If either of them would catch me I would die. After lunch, I took Ginweed to the fairgrounds. She would stay the night there.

August 1 was a very busy day, but I finally got to the fair. Mr. Johnson was the judge. I didn't do much to Ginweed that day except get her some food and water. I was going to be showing against Judy Smith and her Holstein and Tony Davidson and his Holstein. After the show the judge said, "I'm a Holstein man myself, but when you got a Jersey like this, it almost makes me want to change breeds."

That night I slept in the calf house with Ginweed.

The next morning came early, and when I got up, I found Ginweed dead. She had hung herself by falling backward on the rope she was tied to. Dad helped dig her a hole with the tractor. I buried her with the halter and two of the three ribbons she had won. Later that night I went back to her grave. "Ginweed," I said, "we had a heck of a good time together." And I walked away from the grassless patch of earth.

FROM A WRITER'S NOTEBOOK

The Importance of Writing Badly

BRUCE BALLENGER

I was grading papers in the waiting room of my doctor's office one day, and he said, "It must be pretty eye-opening reading that stuff. Can you believe those students had four years of high school and still can't write?"

I've heard that before. I hear it every time I tell a stranger that I teach writing at a university.

I also hear it from colleagues brandishing red pens who hover over their students' papers like Huey helicopters waiting to flush the enemy from the tall grass, waiting for a comma splice or a vague pronoun reference or a misspelled word to break cover.

And I hear it from a commentator on my public radio station who publishes snickering books about how students abuse the sacred language.

I have another problem: getting my students to write badly.

Most of us have lurking in our past some high priest of good grammar whose angry scribbling occupied the margins of our papers. Mine was Mrs.

O'Neill, an eighth-grade teacher with a good heart but no patience for the bad sentence. Her favorite comment on my writing was "awk," which now sounds to me like the grunt of a large bird, but back then meant "awkward." She didn't think much of my sentences.

I find some people who reminisce fondly about their own Mrs. O'Neill, usually an English teacher who terrorized them into worshipping the error-free sentence. In some cases that terror paid off when it was finally transformed into an appreciation for the music a well-made sentence can make.

It didn't work that way with me. I was driven into silence, losing faith that I could ever pick up the pen without breaking the rules or drawing another "awk" from a doubting reader. For years I wrote only when forced to, and when I did it was never good enough. Many of my students come to me similarly voiceless, dreading the first writing assignment because they mistakenly believe that how they say it matters more than discovering what they have to say.

The night before the essay is due they pace their rooms like expectant fathers, waiting for the delivery of the perfect beginning. They wait and they wait and they wait. It's no wonder the waiting finally turns to hating what they have written when they finally get it down. Many pledge to steer clear of English classes, or any class that demands much writing.

My doctor would say my students' failure to make words march down the page with military precision is another example of a failed educational system. There is not enough emphasis on the basics, conservatives argue, despite fifty years of research confirming that knowledge of grammatical structure does not translate into better prose.

Concise, clear writing matters, of course, and I have a responsibility to demand it from my students. But first I am far more interested in encouraging thinking than error-free sentences. That's where bad writing comes in.

When I give my students permission to write badly, to suspend their compulsive need to find "the perfect way of saying it," often something miraculous happens: Words that used to trickle forth come gushing to the page. Students find their voices again, and even more important, they are surprised by what they have to say. They can worry later about fixing awkward sentences. First, they need to make a mess.

It's harder to write badly than you might think. Haunted by their own Mrs. O'Neill, some students can't overlook the sloppiness of their sentences or their lack of eloquence, and quickly stall out and stop writing. When the writing stops, so does the thinking.

The greatest reward in allowing students to write badly is that they learn that language can lead them to meaning, that words can be a means for finding out what they didn't know they knew. It only happens when the words rush to the page, however awkwardly.

I don't mean to excuse bad grammar. But I cringe at conservative educational reformers who believe writing instruction should return to diagramming sentences and referring to Roget's Thesaurus. If policing student papers for mistakes means alienating young writers from the language we expect them to master, then the exercise is self-defeating.

It is more important to allow students to first experience how language can be a vehicle for discovering how they see the world. And what matters in this journey—at least initially—is not what kind of car you're driving, but where you end up.

BRUCE BALLENGER *is the author of six books, five of them on writing, including books in the* Curious *series,* The Curious Researcher, The Curious Reader, *and* The Curious Writer. *He is known for his genius at making the academic and technical both accessible and fascinating. A writer with a strong background in science, Bruce is currently chair of the English Department at Boise State University.*

Six

The Right to See Others Write

Whenever I do writing workshops with teachers, I like to ask, "How many of you saw your own teachers write?" In a group of eighty to one hundred teachers, it is rare for more than two or three hands to go up. Most often, no hands go up at all. Consider what this means. Since so few of us have had formal training in how to teach writing, what we have to fall back on is the modeling that was done for us. And in many cases, that modeling involved assigning, collecting, and correcting writing. It did not involve thinking out loud, talking about where personal writing topics come from, drafting on an overhead or chalkboard, reading an in-process piece aloud (Oh, how I would have *loved* to hear *anything* one of my teachers had written), revising, editing, or even coming up with a title. In other words, we saw our teachers manage and assess, but not write, share, or revise.

If managing and assessing is all we see, that is what we learn to do—at least until we

We breathe, in and out, and some of us trip over things and have funny hair and great shoes and horrible jokes we can't remember the punchlines for and husbands and wives and pets and . . . some of us are scared of spiders. You see, we are live people students can see doing what they are trying to do. And we don't have to do it well! There's no pressure for us to do it well because Cynthia Rylant and Gary Paulsen can do it well. We just have to do it and breathe at the same time. We have to be alive in the room with our students as we write.

—KATIE WOOD RAY
What You Know By Heart

teach ourselves another way. So what does this mean for our students? It means that like most of us, they do not know what writing or revising are supposed to look like. They have to figure it out for themselves. Is this really such a big deal, though? After all, generations of student writers have done this, more or less, with varying degrees of success. Isn't "figuring it out" part of what school is supposed to be about? Perhaps. That's one way of looking at education. But figuring it out works best if you have a lot of time. Years. We do not have that—not really.

The concept that students spend an extended period of their early lives learning to write is an illusion. What we have really, with respect to writing, is an interrupted curriculum and an instructional approach that often varies markedly year to year—so much so that even though students carry numerous skills with them across the grades, shifts in focus (more attention to conventions, less to portfolios) can make it feel as if they are starting over with each new instructor.

Moreover, varied emphasis on writing within districts or within individual classrooms means that many students write as little as once or twice per week. Writing without a sense of continuity is extraordinarily difficult, even for adult professionals, let alone students at the beginning of learning their craft. Donald Graves feels so strongly about this that he advises teachers who can teach writing only one day a week to forget the whole thing rather than frustrate their students:

> If students are not engaged in writing at least four days out of five, and for a period of thirty-five to forty minutes, beginning in first grade, they will have little opportunity to think through the medium of writing. Three days a week are not sufficient. There are too many gaps between the starting and stopping of writing for this schedule to be effective. Only students of exceptional ability, who can fill the gaps with their own initiative and thinking, can survive such poor learning conditions. (1994, 104)

Writing does not lend itself very well to constant starting and stopping. A few minutes here, a few minutes there. We lose our mindset, our momentum. Students—and writers in general—have a need to write for extended periods and to return to their writing frequently.

The fact that time is limited only underscores students' need to see writing in action. Seeing how other people go about it helps us visualize process in our minds, reassures us that we are not alone on days we struggle, and raises possibilities, things to try that we might not think of otherwise. If a picture is worth a thousand words, modeling is worth a thousand pictures. Think of it this way. In teaching our students, we can work at any of four levels:

- Level 1, Assign: *Do this, try that.*
- Level 2, Explain: *Follow these strategies.*
- Level 3, Provide samples: *Here's how writing looks when it's successful.*
- Level 4, Model: *Here's how writing looks as it's going together; here's a strategy that works for me.*

Each time we move to a new level, from assigning to explaining to providing samples to modeling, we dramatically increase the efficiency of instruction. Modeling helps us make the best use of the precious, precious time we have for writing in school. As instructional strategies go, modeling is invaluable.

I'm not suggesting that our students should sit and watch us for hours as we compose whole chapters. But they can frequently watch for, say, fifteen minutes. Here's one thing I do in that amount of time—it illustrates how much information can be shared in even a simple modeling lesson.

Students sometimes have difficulty personalizing an assigned topic. A writer needs to find the catch, the little angle that pertains to *her*. This is a useful thing to model, and it's fast. I ask students to suggest five topics, and I list them at the top of an overhead transparency. Usually one of those topics is immediately appealing, but if none of them grabs me, I'll ask for three more. Then, I choose the topic that speaks to me right then, and explain why it does, and how it relates to my life. Usually, this requires narrowing or focusing the topic.

The students might say, "Write about an animal." I respond by thinking this through out loud, showing them how I talk a broad topic down to size, down to something manageable that I can write about: "The first animal that comes into my head is the neighbor's untrainable dog, Hattie. She is still not housebroken, and frequently gets banished from the house as a result. She feels pretty bad about this. You can usually find her sitting on the back deck—an outcast. When she gives me that forlorn look, I get the feeling she thinks I understand her. What I'd like to write about is the incredibly long, detailed lectures her owners give her, and what I think might be going on in Hattie's Airedale mind as she struggles to figure out what on earth they're talking about—that's where I'll begin."

Then I begin to write on the overhead. I don't talk as I write. I would if I could because I'd like to explain how I'm choosing details or making transitions as I go from one thought to another. But I simply lack the mental dexterity to write and talk at the same time. So I write for a while, and then tell students where I think I'll go next with the writing and why. Then I write again for a time and stop again to talk about it. And so it goes.

After five to ten minutes, I may read what I've written aloud, and then make myself some notes—two or three things I feel I need to do when I return to this piece, things like adding more description, explaining something that's unclear, flipping two passages around, inserting something I've forgotten. Maybe I put a question mark by a sentence or section I'm thinking of deleting. These notes give me a plan to come back to so I don't waste time figuring where I left off or how to begin. Notes save me untold amounts of writing time. And these little ways we find to make writing work for us are, I believe, the most important things we model.

Modeling isn't about pieces of great writing. If I want to show students samples of fine writing, I have a whole world of literature to pull from. Good modeling is about strategies and behaviors. So, what strategies or processes or behaviors have I modeled with this fifteen-minute activity?

- selecting a topic
- personalizing a topic
- narrowing that topic to give it focus
- using what I know, what I think, to create a draft
- reading my writing aloud to see how it flows
- making personal notes to give myself a plan for tomorrow

This little example shows how rich modeling is. We get a lot of instructional value for each moment invested. That's because when we write with and for our students, we teach—even when we don't realize it—multiple things at one time. But where to begin? A novice could spend years with an experienced writer, with a Sandra Cisneros or Barbara Kingsolver or Gary Paulsen, and still not discover all the writer's secrets that person has to share. We cannot model *everything*. So begin with basics, and add some personal touches based on your own experiences and the little things you have taught yourself as a writer.

Writing comes from who we are; modeling must begin with sharing ourselves and what interests *us*—rather than asking students, "What interests *you?*" Instead of interrogating them right off the bat, let's put ourselves on the spot. Let them see who *we* are first, and how that translates into what we write. I love my family and the family stories that have been told at holiday dinners and late-night gatherings over the years. Those stories provide a rich reservoir to which I return again and again, so that's one important thing I can model for students: that we do not exhaust a topic by writing about it. Even when I'm working with an assigned topic, I search for a way to connect it to that internal core: home, family, personal history.

I spent a period of my life as a technical writer, and during that time I wrote student curriculum and teacher guides for several telecourses. One of them was a sociology course, all about family relationships. I loved every minute of the research and the writing. When I wrote about mothers, I was writing about my own mother, or my grandmother, or myself. Being a single mother, balancing career and homemaking, shifting careers, dealing with aging parents and late-life children, dealing with an interfaith marriage, being the center of an extended family: These were the stories of my family, both familiar and fascinating. Every scenario I wrote was peopled with their faces, and the writing flowed effortlessly.

A few months later, I did a similar telecourse on economics. The writing was tortuous. The distance from my personal budget to gross national product was too big a stretch, and while economics clearly affects every person on the planet, I could not find many economists willing to make that connection clear, and so I had to fight my way through both the research and the drafting. Every sentence was a chore. I'd watch the clock inch from ten to twelve, scarcely believing how little I had written. The writing was limp and heavy. My words sounded as if they were coming from someone else. Lack of knowledge, lack of comfort with the topic left me resorting to voiceless generalities: "The impact of the trade deficit on the price of durable goods is significant." Revision was a nightmare. Once I'd written it, I never wanted to see it again.

"You're a writer," a friend told me in rather, I thought, unsympathetic tones. "Writers can write *anything*." Sure. Just as conditioned athletes can play any game. But some are better at basketball than baseball. Writers write best what they know. Writers write best what they love.

In *Conversations*, Regie Routman talks about sharing her passion—literacy—with her students:

> Teachers ask students to write topic after topic, but this is not how I or other writers typically work. As a writer, I do not jump from one subject to another; rather, almost all of my writing is about literacy. It's the topic I'm most passionate about. . . . Yet it is only recently that I have begun sharing that passion with students when I introduce writing. (2000, 296)

One of the greatest gifts we can give our students is helping them discover what they love, too. "Interesting things happen when students find their passion," Routman tells us. "They read and write voraciously about the subject that has captured their attention: They stop asking about length requirements; they stay engaged for long periods of time; their handwriting improves; writing becomes their favorite subject" (296).

What do *you* love most? If you were alone with only your journal to keep you company, what would fill it? Share those things with your students. Let them know where your heart lies.

Sometimes, as with my economics telecourse, we must write about things we find less than fascinating. We do this to make a living or to fulfill an assignment or because state standards dictate that certain requirements pertaining to form or structure or genre must be met. Something good can come of this, though. Today, I often share bits of my economics writing with students so they can see how hard a writer must struggle to find her voice in an unfamiliar landscape. The lesson is "Know your topic." We cannot always write what we know; but (for real-world writing, anyhow) we can *come* to know, through reading and research and observation, the topics about which we need to write. Had

I had more time to do the research I needed to do, to interview economists in person, I would have written with more confidence—hence, more voice.

We also need to model drafting, partly so that students can see how one idea leads into the next—at least in the writer's mind. Thinking—and writing is thinking on paper—is about connecting the dots, after all. It is helpful to see how someone else makes the leap from one sentence or thought or paragraph to another. People do not all draft the same way, and chances are that when your students write, it doesn't look exactly like what you do. For one thing, some people love to compose on a computer, while others prefer to write by hand. The pace is totally different, so whichever you prefer, there's a reason. Some people read aloud as they go; some push on through. Which do *you* do? Show your students, and talk about your style. Let them know it's OK to do it differently. I make notes as I draft. If I know a paragraph is weak, I don't stop to deal with it; instead, I write a note to myself to return to it later. My friend Sneed B. Collard rewrites on the spot. These little differences do not show right or wrong ways of going about writing process. They simply show different approaches that students need to know about if they are to make process work for them.

In modeling drafting, we also model an important writer's habit: *to just sit and write*. This sounds like the easy part; it's anything but. For one thing, it requires *not* doing something else—such as phoning a friend, turning on the television, eating, or taking the dog for a walk. There are thousands of ways to avoid writing—and most writers discover nearly all of them eventually. Writing takes extraordinary concentration. It demands that we shut out the world, however we can—by going to the basement, closing the door, or training ourselves to focus relentlessly.

Some people can write through anything: crying children, thunderstorms, football games, loud appliances, cat fights, or rock music. Though he advises inexperienced writers to tune out every distraction possible, writer Stephen King fully admits to being one of those people who has learned to create his own internal world: "I work to loud music—hard-rock stuff like AC/DC, Guns N' Roses, and Metallica have always been particular favorites—but for me the music is just another way of shutting the door" (2000, 156).

Whatever makes drafting work for *you*, share it with students. Do you need peace and quiet? Tell them. Do you prefer some background music? Play some music to write by for your students. Do you have clutter-phobia? Do you need open space and a bare surface to begin? Natural light? It is impossible in any given classroom to create an ideal environment for all the writers who work there. We can, however, suggest ways of creating a writing retreat somewhere else. A very big part of writing is creating for yourself a place to which you'll want to return. An ambiance conducive to writing.

For me, that takes music (violinist David Wilson playing Cole Porter is heaven on earth, but in a pinch, Randy Newman, Norah Jones, or Ella Fitzgerald will do). It also means books, because I read when I get stuck. I read Garrison Keillor, Barbara Kingsolver, Donald Graves, Anne Lamott, Diane Ackerman, or Bill Bryson. I also work best where I can look out the window periodically. I don't like television or traffic noise. I compose on the computer, but I need lots of sicky notes for marking favorite passages, and pads to scribble on. One of my writer friends likes to work outside, using a portable computer. One likes to sit near an aquarium and be surrounded by potted plants. Another likes the cat on her lap. You and your students can have a good time talking about the ideal writing environment. Maybe you can't create it in your classroom, but you can describe it. And at the very least, this could suggest for students how very terrific it would be if they created for themselves, somewhere in the world, a personal writing space, however humble. Writers don't need a desk from Pottery Barn, but they do need a place to go.

Two other things students need to see modeled are sharing and revising. Sharing is important because for many people (teachers included) it is frightening. So what we model is not so much the technique of sharing as the courage to share. We need to read our writing unapologetically. Instead of beginning with "This is only a draft," we can start by asking for the response we'd like: "Tell me what you see in your mind as I read," or "Tell me your impression of the character called Sam." This gives the audience something to listen *for*, which makes them much more comfortable, too. Listeners often feel as tense as the writer. They don't know what they are supposed to say. They are especially afraid of not liking the writer's work and then having to come up with a pleasant comment. As writers, we need to put our listeners at ease by telling them what kind of help we need. We also need to read our writing with plenty of voice. To be daring. If we do this, we tell students it's OK for them to do it, too—and only animated reading will allow them to hear the voice in their own writing.

In modeling revision, be bold. Slash and burn. Use arrows and bubble inserts and cross-outs. Cut and paste if you need to. Read aloud as you go. Ask students for their advice: "Which sounds better?" Make a mess so they can see that restructuring a sentence or cutting a whole paragraph are things writers do. If you get stuck, write a note to yourself or pose a question in the margin you can come back to later: *More detail needed here.* When I'm finished for the day, I always write myself a note in capital letters so I can find it in a hurry: YOU ARE HERE. Then I have the option to go back to the beginning or start my next day's revision in the middle. Think of all the pieces of writing that are just stellar beginning to middle, but fade into monotony middle to end. Did you ever wonder why this is? It's because most writers go back to the beginning when they revise, and the more tired they get, the more easily satisfied they are;

by the time they get to the end, they're reasonably happy with everything. We need to model the enormous revisional advantage of beginning in the middle.

When we model revision, I think it's also helpful if we truly like our writing. It's often better than we think it is, and even when that's not true, it usually has potential students will uncover. Revision is about change, not mutilation. When your hair gets mussed, you don't shave your head. Students conditioned by grades on final drafts may need permission to love writing that's still in process—the very writing that needs our love the most. Sometimes I think we hesitate to show anyone our unfinished writing because we feel like first-day enrollees at a nudist camp. There's just *so* much to apologize for, plus everyone is staring. Actually, students are, in my experience, extremely kind about teachers' writing. They feel just as we do during conferences. They want *so much* to say something helpful. They want to say the *very thing* that will help you turn a writing corner. Let them know what you need, and in doing so, you teach them to be gentle with themselves as they revise.

One very useful way to go about modeling, I believe, is to let students see you take a piece of writing that is personally important to you through the entire process. This may take several days, or—in the case of a more complex piece— even several weeks. As you work, personalize the process every step of the way. Talk about how *you* found this topic (or how it found you), how much you know and how much you'll have to research, whether you'll write the first draft in one sitting or over a period of time, whether revision is something you dread or look forward to, whether you plan to share it or keep it to yourself until it's finished, and so forth. Save what you write, revise, or edit—*all* drafts. That way, at the end, not only will you have shared many of your personal writer's secrets, but your students will have a visual record of your journey.

One thing students learn from watching us model process is that writing is mostly about problem solving. Invite students to share in this problem solving process by being coaches for you. If you do this, modeling becomes a team effort instead of a solo performance, and students' participation increases their engagement as well as their understanding.

Now and then we need a little moral support from other writers. No problem. It's all right there in the books we love: striking imagery, good use of verbs, authentic dialogue, strong voice, and much more. Katie Wood Ray calls the authors of these books "our co-teachers of writing." These people, she reminds us, "sit on our bookshelves and in our magazine baskets patiently waiting to show our students and us great writing moves" (2002, 3). I think of them as literary mentors, writers whose work is so fine that literally every page provides a lesson of the craft. When we share their work and discuss it with our students, it isn't *quite* like having these people come into classrooms and model for us—but it's the next best thing, especially if we try to imagine the work behind the text.

Suppose you could invite four literary mentors into your own classroom. Who would they be? As you think about that, let me tell you about four I would like to observe doing a modeling lesson, and what my imagination tells me I *might* learn from watching each one.

My first choice would be Annie Proulx, whose eye for detail is unsurpassed and whose wit is as dry as the Texas panhandle of which she writes in *That Old Ace in the Hole*:

> After thirty months of toil with boxes and broken glass and miniscule annual raises he had had an unfortunate experience with the company's president, Mrs. Eudora Giddins, widow of Millrace Giddins who had founded the company. He was fired. And he was glad, for he did not want life to be a kind of fidgety waiting among lightbulbs, as for a report card. He wanted to aim at a high mark on a distant wall. (2002, 5)

Life as "a kind of fidgety waiting among lightbulbs" is poetry, a frugal use of words to convey worlds of meaning. I love the phrase "a high mark on a distant wall" because I think that's exactly what most of us aim for. Did Annie Proulx come up with this word choice right off the bat—or if not, how many drafts did that passage take? Model that for me, Annie. Oh, how I wish you could.

I would also love to watch novelist Richard Peck modeling the concept of real-world research. I chose Peck because he writes with such honesty, and there is no substitute for that in writing—none. He begins his book *Invitations to the World* with a confession:

> I learned to be a teacher as I was to learn to be a writer, where I was already on the job, the only adult in the room, and the door was closed between me and all help. In teaching I thought I'd found my true calling because it made me laugh and cry and kept me up at night. Like writing. (2002)

Peck's book deals very directly with the question "Where do you get your ideas?" The source of our thinking is one of the most valuable things we can model. I get the sense Peck has been asked this question so many times that finally he said, "Enough. I'll just put it in a book, and then you can buy the book." As he explains, ideas come from life, and so living is a kind of research, a process of which we need to be more conscious:

> All fiction writing depends on the amassing of a lunatic amount of observable material. I was gathering material long before I knew what

to do with it. Writers and children are natural snoops, though writers call it "research." Had I known how brief childhood is, I'd have looked closer. (17)

We usually associate research with nonfiction writing—and here is one of our mentors reminding us that it is equally important for fiction. Perhaps a character like the irascible but tender-hearted Andy Sipowicz of *NYPD Blue* evolves because the writer that created him once knew a police officer who feared written tests or liked reading to his children or had an affinity for tropical fish. Andy seems real to millions of viewers because a "natural snoop" took some "observable material" and used it to bring a television cop to life.

My third choice is Anne Lamott, because she has discovered something most of us have not: the power of being gentle with yourself as a writer. I would like to see her model this very thing. I would like to see what writing looks as it flows from the pen or the keyboard of someone who offers me this suggestion: "Try looking at your mind as a wayward puppy that you are trying to paper train. You don't drop-kick a puppy into the neighbor's yard every time it piddles on the floor. You just keep bringing it back to the newspaper" (1995, 99).

Most of us aren't as good at modeling as we could be because we're too uptight about it. We are drop-kicking that puppy right and left because we think modeling is mostly (not totally, but *mostly*) about getting it right. We're not into showing students how it's done so much as showing them how it looks when it's *done well*.

We visualize ourselves striding to the overhead projector with the sort of confidence that only comes from inner genius. But then, just as we're about to dazzle the troops with wisdom and insight, the editor in our heads takes over, reminding us that we're not as smart as we thought we were: "So, Mighty Modeler of Writing, what are we writing about today? Ah, yes, your first time driving. In case you'd forgotten, *everyone* writes about that. Bo-o-oring." Lamott has learned to punt this editor into the next county where she belongs, and to believe in the inherent generative power of writing. We keep going even if we can't yet see where we're headed. We drive right on through the fog and sleet and rain because what we're heading for is not the Pulitzer, but just a page with some text on it. If we keep one foot on the gas, we will get there.

Another of my writing mentors is Natalie Goldberg, my fourth choice because when I read her books, I feel as if we're sitting down for a chat. Like Lamott, she acknowledges the messiness of writing. Messiness *can* be a result of unclear thinking, but it's also the normal state for writing in process, and it increases in direct proportion to the length and complexity of the writing. If I am writing a letter, for example, I have little trouble finishing it because it's short and compact. Its focus is small. A book is another creature altogether.

It's unwieldy. It sprawls out, sending runners in many directions at once. I write one chapter and what I've written makes me see another chapter differently. The more I write, the quicker I must be to keep all these tendrils within the fragile boundaries of my garden. And there's another problem, too, which is to make nine chapters look and feel as if they were written by one person instead of a nine-person committee. It's hard but possible, Goldberg reassures me, to bring big writing together under one roof:

> Structure is a tricky and important business. I tried to write *Bones* eight years before I actually wrote it. Back then, I just couldn't figure out how to set it up. I seemed to be just scattering bricks, helter-skelter. It was almost as if I couldn't figure out how to put up the walls, lift the roof on the house. So I quit. . . . Eight years later, I flashed on the idea of short chapters, each one a separate entity. (1990, 16)

Books do not go together, page by page, in order. Not usually, anyway. Instead, they are assembled much the way films are made. That means the "final scene" may be shot first. Later, all the pieces are brought together and reassembled in a way that tells a story or makes a point.

A piece of writing is a slippery thing, looking and sounding quite different when we pull it from the file than it did ten days before when we felt so good, so satisfied, tucking it away. What has changed? Not the writing, but ourselves. We have gained perspective, distance, and the insight that comes from living with a topic in your head. Picasso once said that a picture "lives a life like a living creature." It is not simply thought up and then put onto paper as if the artist's thoughts were being photocopied. Instead, he tells us, "While it is being done it changes as one's thoughts change. And when it is finished, it still goes on changing, according to the state of mind of whoever is looking at it" (Clark 1993, 12). So it is with writing.

In the chapter called "Fresh Writing," Goldberg talks about the circular process she uses to shape her own writing, a process through which she becomes her own writing coach:

> I leave my initial writing for a week or so, to get some distance from it before I reread it. Then when I reread it, if I see I should have said more about Nell's brown hat, I write the letter A and circle it where I want to add that additional material. Then on a separate page, I put an A at the top. I say, "Go Nat, ten minutes on Nell's hat." I return over and over to writing practice. This continually allows me to come back to fresh writing, even in revisions. When I type it up, I'll insert A where it belongs. (1990, 60–61)

Notice what a small thing this is, yet how ingenious. Suppose Goldberg were to model this very practice in a writing workshop. What would she be teaching us, her students?

1. Leave writing alone for some time to get mental distance.
2. Reread what you have written.
3. If there's something missing, mark it, but keep reading.
4. Write inserts on a separate page, so the writing will be fresh.
5. Give yourself time limits so revision doesn't become tedious.

The secret to good modeling is to notice the tiny things we do as writers and to share them with our students. Too often we overlook these practices because we may think, "Oh, they know that—*everyone* knows that." Everyone does not know the value of leaving writing alone for a time and letting your thoughts regroup. Everyone does not know the value of reading writing aloud, even if you just read to the plant in the corner. Everyone does not know the value of marking text for little inserts to make the revision more powerful. Or timing yourself so you push a little.

Think of the things you do as a writer that make the process work for *you*. Write them down. Those are the things you need to model for your students. Let your students in on the secrets. Bernard Malamud once said, "I think it hurts a writer to have his secrets known . . . so much depends on one's ability to maintain illusion" (Brodie 1997, 44). Every one of my teachers through twelfth grade must have had this quotation taped to his or her desk. For a long while, writing has been taught just this way, as a series of illusions. It is time to let students come backstage.

If they're lucky, students may get an opportunity to observe favorite writers modeling some of the secrets to the craft. Gary Paulsen might drop by to explain how he gets by with such long sentences; Sandra Cisneros might talk about how she makes repetition work for and not against her; perhaps Garrison Keillor could talk about making fictional characters seem real; Sneed B. Collard could show us how long a nonfiction writer can go, safely, without a story—and still hang onto his audience; Diane Ackerman could share a lesson on verbs; and Samantha Abeel could show us how, in revising writing, you summon the courage to tell the absolute truth and how that courage gives your writing voice.

Don't forget that even if we do not schedule author visits, our students have resident writers from whom to learn. They have us. And we have more to teach than we might think. Here are a few simple things I've learned as a writer that I could model, and have modeled, for students. Your own list will be better because it's yours, but this will give you ideas to work from:

- writing the title last
- double spacing to give myself room to breathe
- asking someone else to read the piece aloud so I can hear it in another voice
- stopping in the middle of a sentence or paragraph, to help jump start my writing tomorrow
- cutting what doesn't fit—even if I really like it
- writing to music because it helps me concentrate
- watching out for repeated words (we all have favorites) that deaden the writing
- watching out for *very, really,* and *actually,* words that can creep into every sentence
- writing a conclusion that reads like the beginning of a new piece
- reading everything I write aloud
- starting my revision in the middle sometimes
- avoiding long sentences—they're too hard to follow (and I'm not Gary Paulsen)
- avoiding adverbs if a stronger verb will make them unnecessary
- thinking, when I'm stuck, what I would say to the reader if she were sitting right there, and then writing *that*
- pulling out Lamott or Goldberg or Peck or Proulx when the words just won't come, opening the book at random, and spending a few minutes with a good writing mentor

What idea lives in your head right now itching to find its way to the page? Take it to the next step, whatever that might be for you. Talk about it, draw a picture, share photographs, make a list or web or outline, do a sketchy rough draft. Then write. You don't have to compose every inch of the piece in front of an audience, but compose some of it as students watch.

Read what you write aloud. Like Natalie Goldberg, make yourself some marginal notes. Give yourself suggestions and assignments and encouraging words. Be compassionate, like Anne Lamott; forgive yourself for not being perfect and give yourself permission to be a writer anyhow. As you revise, imagine Richard Peck is peeking over your shoulder, nudging you to notice more. *Do* that. Make every detail count. Take a hint from Annie Proulx and insert some authentic dialogue. Listen to the voice emerge, and don't forget to thank Annie for that tip. Remember Picasso's words and remind yourself that what you are creating is not a snapshot, but a living, breathing document that changes with your thinking and with that of your students.

No one experiences writing process quite as you do. So the lessons you provide for your students are unique, unavailable elsewhere. No one else has your writing topics, your voice, your favorite words, your way with imagery, your sense of rhythm, your command of conventions. You can be selfish about these things and maintain the illusion of writing as magic, but why should you? Maya Angelou once said that you can learn a lot about a person by the way he or she handles these three things: rainy days, lost luggage, and tangled Christmas lights. You can also learn a lot by how someone handles writing. Let your students see how you do it.

FROM A WRITER'S NOTEBOOK

Let's Be Honest

JIM BURKE

Writing—the *doing* of it—keeps me honest when it comes to writing—the *teaching* of it. On occasion, I will cook up some writing assignment I think is just *so* good, so smart, so effective—until the kids' papers start coming in. That's when it hits me that I didn't think the assignment through, didn't test it out myself first.

At such moments, teachers have two choices: We can hide behind our authority and start chiding the troops for a failed mission, or get into the trenches with our students to see what went wrong. What we find if we look long enough and if we are honest is that we could not do much better ourselves. That idea we thought was so brilliant turns out to be too complex, or too vague, or it has too many working parts. Such failures bring to mind a favorite writers' dictum: *Always kill your darlings first*—which is to say, if you think an assignment is great, it probably needs more work than you are willing to admit. We would discover this quickly enough if we gave *ourselves* assignments more often.

Writing is hard work; writing well is even harder. I didn't realize this until I wrote my first article as a teacher-author. I had seen a long article on a day in the life of a nurse, and thought people should know what a day in the life of a student teacher was like. So I set about writing what turned out to be a four thousand–word article. It was the first thing I had ever written about my work, and the experience woke me up in a profound way. A man named Michael Harris at the *San Francisco Chronicle* read my piece and subsequently returned it, saying he thought it would make a great essay if only I would trim it down—by about 3,000 words! Thus began my process of becoming not just a writer, but a more effective teacher of writing.

One of the words most associated with writing—*text*—relates to textiles, to weaving. It is hard to imagine teaching someone to weave without having a personal feeling for the act. Teachers need not be published authors, but they must be able to speak from a place of knowing, to have the experience—regularly—of struggling to solve textual problems. Without such fluency, such experience with their own process, they cannot expect to understand the problems student writers face or to help those students develop their own personal writing process.

When I am writing an article or book, I typically keep portions of it with me to read, reflect upon, or work on (between classes, at stop lights, during faculty meetings). These pages have notes in the margins, arrows directing me to move words to other spots, and sticky notes filled with whole new passages to be woven in later. I emphasize for students the importance of getting what Donald Murray calls a "down draft" so I can get busy shaping the words, the syntax, the organization, and so on. In the end, this experience with my own writing forces me to pay attention to what writers need, what *I* need if I am to write well. Writing keeps me honest.

I want my students to demand, as I do, their right to wander within a topic—for the word *essay* means *to try*, which is to say, to explore in an attempt to understand a subject. I want them to demand their right, as I do, to write about ideas and subjects they choose and that matter to them. And I want them to insist on their right to learn from someone who understands the complexities of the craft they are struggling to master, someone who has struggled himself and has achieved, through that struggle, the kind of insider's wisdom that translates into better instruction—*and* better writing.

JIM BURKE *teaches English at Burlingame High School in California. He is the author of numerous best-selling books, including* The English Teacher's Companion, Second Edition, The Teacher's Daybook, Tools for Thought, Reading Reminders, *and* Writing Reminders, *all published by Heinemann, as well as* The Reader's Handbook, *published by Great Source. Jim is the recipient of NCTE's 2000 Exemplary English Leadership Award and was inducted into the California Reading Association's Hall of Fame in 2001. He currently serves on the Adolescence and Young Adulthood/English Language Arts Standards Committee of the National Board for Professional Teaching Standards.*

Seven
The Right to Be Assessed Well

Ours is a nation obsessed with assessment. We assess our students continuously, and while it is a very good thing to establish accountability and to see how things are going, constant assessment also carries with it a heavy price, one that is dramatically inflated when assessment is not all that it could be.

One thing that happens in an assessment-heavy environment is that inordinate amounts of time are devoted to preparing for "the test." A teacher friend told me last October, "We're finished with boot camp. That's what we call it when we have finished the six weeks it takes to prepare for the test." Six weeks is a big slice from the normal curriculum. I wonder whether the parents and others who applaud testing as a means of ensuring quality in our schools are at all uneasy about making test preparation a curriculum unto itself. Then there's the related question of why we feel compelled to teach something

The trouble with moral statistics is that every generation concentrates on measuring what it is most afraid of. But because it is impossible to measure what is most important—you can't measure love, morals, or health—they have to make do with what is easiest to measure. So [the British civil servant] Chadwick and his fellow early statisticians used to measure . . . the spirituality of children by how many hymns they could recite by heart. Not the same thing at all.

—DAVID BOYLE AND
ANITA RODDICK
Numbers

special, something totally separate from the usual writing workshop, in order to prepare for the test. Some would argue that the tests are identifying for us what is most critical, that it is not always a match with our curriculum—and that perhaps it should be. Are we sure about that? Or is it more the case that tests themselves should be revised so that they are more closely aligned with what teachers and other educators *know* is critical? In the case of writing assessment, the latter is often closer to the truth.

Student writers are assessed at three basic levels: at the state or district level, where teachers may or may not play a central role in assessing students' work; at the classroom level, where teachers are the primary assessors; and at the personal level, where students themselves assess their own work. In each case, students have a right to the highest quality assessment our understanding of writing and writing process can provide. Being assessed well in the world of writing means three things.

First, it requires that the assessment be perceptive. The *perceptive* response is not the same as the *right* response—not exactly. Some questions have a right answer: *What is the capital of Venezuela? What is the speed of light?* But the question *What are the strengths and weaknesses of this piece of writing?* has no right answers. It does, however, have relatively perceptive versus superficial answers. Perceptive assessment demands careful, reflective reading of a piece, together with a writer's perspective acquired through years of reading and writing. Such assessment goes beyond cosmetics to the underlying meaning and structure, and may even call up in the reader's head a pretty good approximation of the original writer's voice. Good assessors sense the heartbeat behind the words.

Second, quality assessment is compassionate. By that I mean that it seeks not to find fault, but to uplift—to genuinely *help* writers. So much of assessment is about identifying problems. But courage is what writers need most. Courage is of more enduring value than any writing technique or strategy. Therefore, *encouragement*, or the bolstering of that courage, is what we as teachers and writing coaches ought to provide. If I am trying to push a large rock up a hill, the last thing I need is for someone to tell me I probably won't make it—or by how many feet I will miss the mark. For many student writers, the hill feels steep and the rock is growing heavier by the minute. In that situation, courage is all that stands between that student and giving up. (See Figures 7–1 and 7–2.)

The message "You cannot write well" or "You are not meeting the standard" is hollow unless it's accompanied by the comfort of a second message: "Don't worry—I can show you *just* what to do about it." In the book *Because Writing Matters*, National Writing Project (NWP) authors point out that "For teachers and students, assessment should have an instructional purpose, not simply an evaluative or administrative one. That is, it should identify and diagnose a specific problem in student writing or adjust a lesson plan to meet student needs as they are uncovered" (2003, 76–77).

Third, quality assessment is useful. I do not mean useful to data gatherers eager to report on perceived growth, decline, or stagnation. Rather, I am talking about its usefulness to the people assessment should be designed to serve first and foremost: student writers. In this spirit, we must ensure that assessment at every level helps students to identify not only needs to be

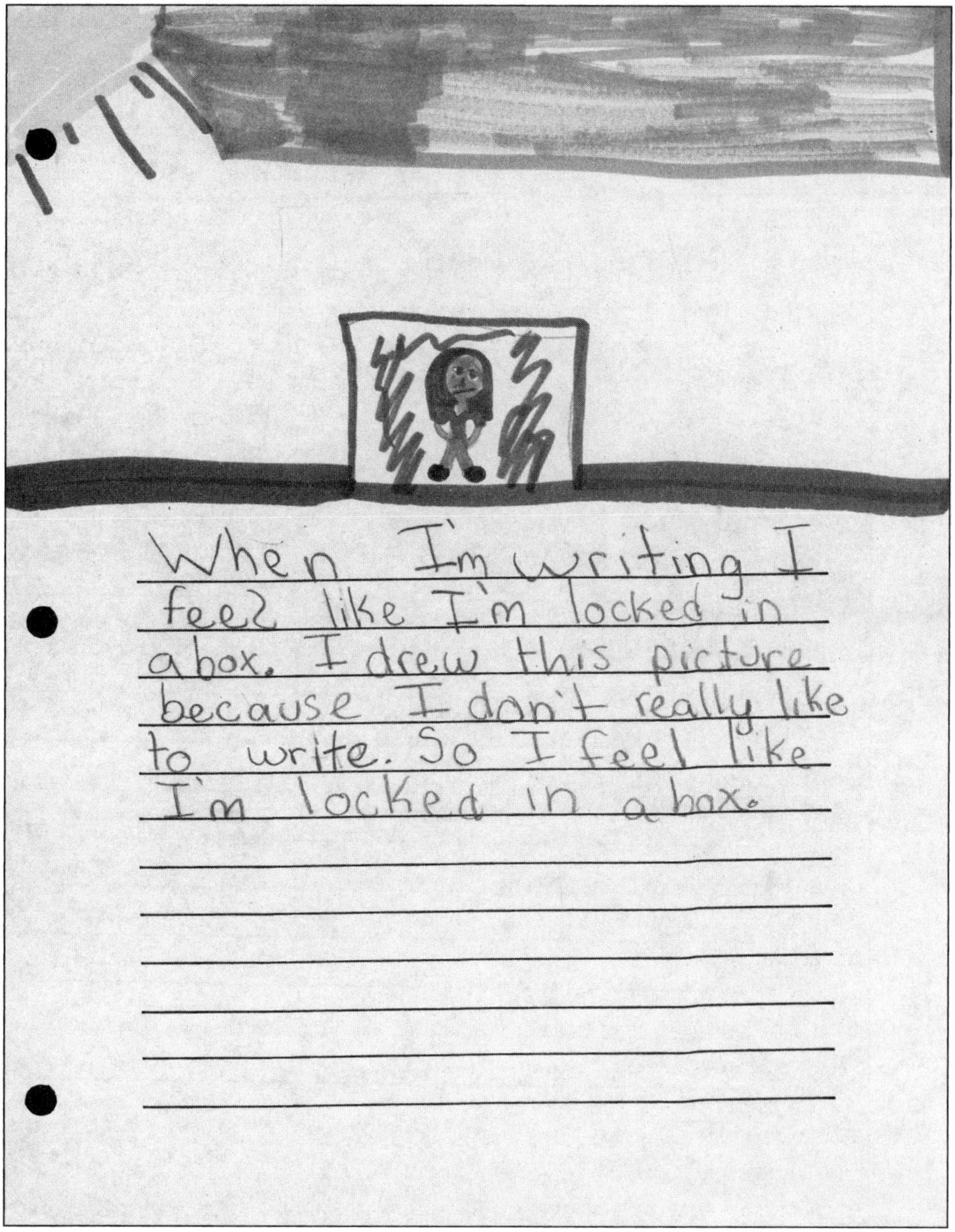

When I'm writing I feel like I'm locked in a box. I drew this picture because I don't really like to write. So I feel like I'm locked in a box.

FIGURE 7–1

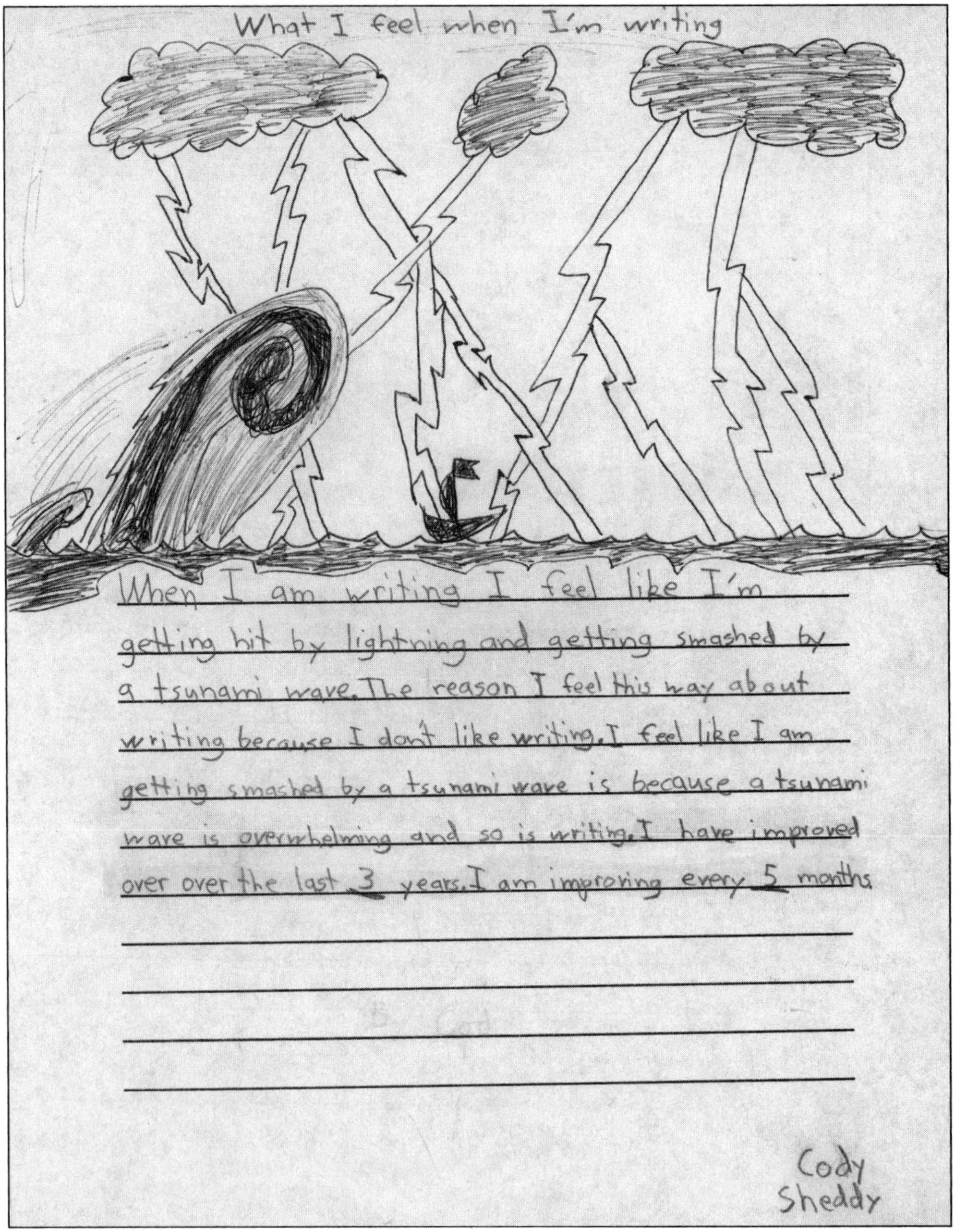

What I feel when I'm writing

When I am writing I feel like I'm getting hit by lightning and getting smashed by a tsunami wave. The reason I feel this way about writing because I don't like writing. I feel like I am getting smashed by a tsunami wave is because a tsunami wave is overwhelming and so is writing. I have improved over over the last 3 years. I am improving every 5 months

Cody Sheddy

FIGURE 7–2

addressed but, even more important, strengths to build upon. Second grader Ben had written a piece so lyrical his teacher could not resist sharing it with her colleagues:

> Somewhere in a time that's been, somewhere on earth, there lived a small pipe rat. (Fraser and Skolnick 1994, 121)

The teacher knew why Ben's piece was so wonderful. Her colleagues knew. *Everyone* knew—except Ben, the person who needed that insight the most. "Please, Mrs. Skolnick," he said, "would you tell me what I did right in my story so I can do it again?" Like Ben, many student writers have strengths upon which to build. But they need to know first that this is so, and second, what their strengths are.

Good assessment does not come about by accident. It is the result of clear vision and thoughtful planning. Following are some features that define quality writing assessment at the large-scale (state or district), classroom, and individual levels, features to help ensure that assessment and instruction work in harmony.

Large-scale writing assessment is most often an attempt to measure whether and to what extent students are meeting writing standards set by the state. This is a worthy goal, especially if the standards reflect what is truly important in good writing: thoughtful development of ideas, organizational structure that guides the reader through a discussion, individual voice that moves us as readers, and skill-fully used conventions that enhance both voice and meaning. When such assessment is designed with care and implemented with sensitivity, it can have immeasurable impact on the shape and force of writing instruction.

A case in point is the assessment conducted by the state of Kentucky, which has shifted, just since 1990, from an emphasis on the "expedient five-paragraph theme" (National Writing Project 2003, 83) to a combination of on-demand and portfolio writing that spans genres, themes, and purposes, and includes writing produced for classes other than English. Kentucky's assessment allows students extended time to plan their writing and gives them a sense of ownership because they select the writing for the portfolio and also prepare a letter to reviewers reflecting on their work (83).

Researcher George Hillocks Jr., who has looked closely at writing assessments across the country, cites Kentucky's assessment as innovative and effective because "it provides . . . time for students to develop pieces of writing adequately so that they do not have to revert to the formulaic" (NWP 2003, 85). He also points out that fully 80 percent of Kentucky teachers "feel that the portfolio assessment has helped improve writing in the state" (85).

Most states would be hard-pressed to come anywhere close to that level of teacher endorsement, but consider what Kentucky's state assessors have done to earn such trust. First, they have placed solid faith in writing process as the foundation of good writing, giving students significant amounts of time to design their writing, to produce it, and later to reflect upon it and reshape it. Second, they have given more than lip service to what research has repeatedly demonstrated, that "multiple samples of student work, each written for a distinct audience and purpose, can give a much deeper sense of a writer's abilities and developmental needs" than any single snapshot approach (NWP 2003, 78). We need to acknowledge that we use the snapshot approach to save ourselves time, trouble, and money, and not because it is a good (or even adequate) way to assess writing.

Third—and this is the part that impresses me most—Kentucky has shown great respect for its student writers. These students, assessed at grades four, seven, and twelve, are asked to design their own portfolios, selecting those pieces of work *they* feel best reflect who they are as writers. Surely there cannot be a moment when assessment and instruction come together better than this. In reviewing her work, a student relives her journey as a writer. She learns to read with a critic's eye and a writer's understanding. No other single experience can put her more securely in control of her own writing process.

Unfortunately, not every state is—as yet—following Kentucky's lead. Hillocks' research suggests that in some states, on-demand writing assessment provides students with as little as forty minutes' response time, allows no interaction among students, and in general bears minimal resemblance to the process-based approach of the classroom (NWP 2003, 189). This has three implications.

First, it makes the assessment process unfamiliar and uncomfortable to students, who wonder why they are assessed in a way so markedly different from the way in which writing is taught. Second, it forces us to question whether the writing produced under such conditions represents or even approaches students' best efforts. Third—and this is the real danger—because assessment has such impact upon instruction, it may persuade some educators to spend less time on complex writing tasks such as self-selection of topics, research, portfolio creation, or in-depth revision, and more time training students to be comfortable with the quick-write formulaic response they are likely to see on the assessment. "Teachers teach what is on the test and ignore what is not," Hillocks cautions (NWP 2003, 204). We should be very, very careful what we assess, for in the end, what we assess is what we will get.

Many large-scale assessments pay only modest homage to writing process. They ask students to "Think carefully before you write" (a nod to prewriting) and to "Look over your writing before turning your paper in" (a nod to revision). In neither case does the process look anything like what most teachers would like to see happen in the classroom. True, things are improving slowly—and not only in Kentucky. For example, some states, such as Alaska, now allow students as much time as they would like to complete their writing, and while single-shot assessment can never rival the portfolio approach for measuring depth or breadth of writing skill, this is still a breakthrough. In addition, many assessments allow access to basic resources, such as a dictionary.

There remains one issue, though, on which large-scale assessors are reluctant to budge: their insistence that the writer work *alone*. We might refer to this fear of consulting or conferencing as *collaboraphobia*, or the irrational fear that human contact of any kind is tantamount to cheating. People who suffer from collaboraphobia have, I suspect, limited experience writing—*or* working with student response groups. If the creation of superb writing meant you had only to check with a partner, teaching writing would be a lot simpler, and we would all be walking around with Pulitzer prizes under our arms.

In the real world of writing, some writers actually like solitude, and refuse to allow anyone even a glimpse of their work until it is ready to print. Many, however, share writing with family or friends or editors all the time, seek suggestions, and revise accordingly. No one whispers behind a pillar at the debut of a first novel, "Well, she didn't really write that book *herself*, you know. I have it on good authority that she read several chapters aloud to friends." Good for her—if that helps. Assessors should know that it does not help everyone.

In the classroom, student writers confer with the teacher or another writing coach and share their writing with partners or in a small group. Collaboration does not, sad to say, guarantee success: *Confer and publish!* It only provides the writer with new jumping off points. The writer must still know how to make use of the responses she receives. Not all advice is good or even helpful. Writers must learn to sift through the trivia and find the gems. Even then, the leap from receiving commentary to crafting meaningful text is huge. Writing assessments are not like quiz shows, where answers can be smuggled in. They are not tests of memory. They are tests of *applied skill*. In the end, despite everything, the writer is alone with her blank sheet of paper. She couldn't be more alone if we stuck her atop a mesa in Monument Valley.

What we really need to know is how well our students can perform when they make use of *every resource available to them*, including reader response. We should also pause a moment to consider what students might gain from the assessment process itself if part of their responsibility included responding to the work of others. We should be doing everything possible to build thinking skills into the assessment process; this would be one way to do that.

It's common these days to send writing assessment samples out of state to testing companies where they are read by teams of readers, not all of whom may be teachers—or writers. What a lost professional development opportunity for teachers. The chance to work with colleagues and to read hundreds, sometimes thousands, of student samples can show teachers in a way nothing else can just where students are succeeding and where they are struggling. This information is invaluable in designing instruction. Maddie Brick, ELA coordinator for Hudson Schools, notes that "you get some pretty dramatic results when you get teachers in conversations that are deep and built around common expectations and standards" (NWP 2003, 98). Many teachers will tell you that serving as a rater for a large-scale assessment is one of the most valuable (albeit, exhausting) professional development experiences they have had.

Whether they're teachers or not, what do we have a right to ask of reviewers who score student work? For one thing, they should be readers. People who feel at home within books approach writing differently. They are more likely to hear the voice, to follow the writer's trail, and to decode the message quickly because they have had so much practice at it. It's what they do all the time. It's what they love. Experienced readers do not depend on formula; they don't even like it. They want to dance without looking at the painted footprints. They are comfortable with subtlety and with lack of structure, and in their hands the more sophisticated writers, those who produce more complex text, tend to be rewarded for their efforts. People who read for the sheer joy of it also appreciate the many forms writing can take. They like diversity; they appreciate surprises. So they reward individuality as well. Furthermore, they have endurance. This is critical. The student whose paper is read at 2:00 P.M. should not receive lower scores because the reviewer was exhausted.

Reviewers should also be writers. People who write are appropriately and unabashedly impressed by the talents of other writers. They are unafraid to give a mental standing ovation for fear a better performance will come along. And that's as it should be. They are also troubled when a skilled writer takes an obvious shortcut: *Now you know the three reasons I loved Uncle Bill*. And that's as it should be, too. Writers also recognize when another writer is taking a risk—just the way an Olympic judge who is a skater himself knows when a competitive skater is putting herself in peril for the sake of the performance. Writers value risk-taking by other writers.

Finally, reviewers should be able to put personal preferences aside and judge writing on its merits. Length, appearance, topic, or other factors unrelated to the quality of the writing should not influence scores. We all have pet peeves. We may dislike loopy writing, football stories, a sarcastic tone, or a blatant disregard for margins. Fair enough. But usually these are not the qualities on which we are asked to assess writing performance. Good reviewers respect the requirements of the standards or the rubric that forms the basis of the assessment.

Of course, this assumes that the rubric itself is sound, and that is a very big assumption. Many rubrics are vague or inconsistent; they address one set of concerns at the top level, another midlevel, and still another at the beginning level. Many encourage formulaic writing because formulaic rubrics that depend on quantitative criteria (numbers of supporting details, numbers of complex sentences) are relatively easy to construct and apply. Some use very negative language to define beginning-level performance, or rely on qualitative terms like *fair* or *poor* or *excellent* to describe performance—as opposed to terms like *beginning*, *developing*, and *strong*. Such rubrics tend to imply that performance at upper levels is nearly perfect, while that at beginning levels is hopeless. Neither is true. We don't want our writers, not one of them, to think of themselves as poor performers. This is counterproductive. We want those who put even a single line on paper to think of themselves as having made a start. We want those at the top to recognize they still have room to grow.

Quality rubrics have several characteristics that command respect. First, they are clear. The language used to define performance is easy to understand, not just for teachers, but for students. In addition, the language identifies problems or strengths in the writing; it does not point fingers at or lavish praise upon the writer. If an issue such as detail or sentence length is addressed at one level, it is addressed at *all* levels. In addition, quality rubrics reflect what is truly important in writing—all writing, not just that created within the classroom. Rubrics mirror what we value, so it is important that we not leave out what we care about.

Over the last few years, I have often been asked whether it is a good idea to assess the trait of voice. This question is driven by the concern that voice is too subjective to evaluate fairly. Voice *is* subjective, true. That's no sign we shouldn't tackle it if we believe it is important. Other qualities of writing are subjective, too.

Consider idea development: Some readers like an explicit thesis that appears in the first paragraph, while others are much happier with an implicit thesis that is never stated outright. Some are satisfied with broad-brush detail: *The forest was a mix of tall evergreens and low-growing shrubs.* That's more precise than *The forest was thick.* Still, some readers want the picture brought into sharper focus: *Two hundred-year-old Ponderosas rose one hundred and fifty feet or more from their red puzzle-like bark hugging trunks as broad as dining tables; between these giants, where the sun found a path to the heavily needled forest floor, the thick low-growing manzanita bushes created dense mounds of shiny green leaves and soft pink flowers, light as feathers.* Which of these is "best" is a matter of taste, and how your taste runs determines which writer gets the highest score.

Nor is that the end of it. Some readers prefer their details organized neatly, like items about to be packed for a long trip: first detail, second detail, final detail. Others (maybe those who pack on impulse) are happier with a random mix. They like the occasional odd detail that pops up like the passport somebody left next to the toaster. It is also fair to say that readers frequently favor both topics and opinions that echo their own thinking or reflect their own preferences. The story of a twelve-inning baseball game plays best to fans of the sport.

Subjectivity even affects our response to conventions. Readers disagree, sometimes vehemently, about whether to begin sentences with *And* or *But*, about how many commas to use in a series, whether contractions are acceptable in a formal report, whether fragments are allowable or even stylistically desirable, whether *that* and *which* are ever interchangeable (ditto *can* and *may*), whether *geopolitical* or *well-done* should be hyphenated, and a thousand other things you can list for yourself. Not all of us are equally up-to-date on our conventions, and to complicate the issue, conventions are continually changing, making handbooks obsolete almost as quickly as they can be printed.

Subjectivity isn't evil; it's just human. To omit voice on the grounds that it is a subjective trait is prejudicial. All writing qualities are subjective. I was particularly struck by this comment from assessment specialist Grant Wiggins:

> Many state writing assessments run the risk of undercutting good writing by scoring only for focus, organization, style, and mechanics without once asking judges to consider whether the writing is powerful, memorable, provocative, or moving (all impact-related criteria, and all at the heart of why people read what others write). (NWP 2003, 78)

Look again at Wiggins' words: "powerful, memorable, provocative, or moving." What gives writing these qualities? Voice. The very things, Wiggins tells us, that are "at the heart of why people read what others write." Voice is the point. It's the reason for the reading. It's the reason we buy and publish books, remember what we read, or preserve what we write. Should we include voice in our rubrics? Absolutely. Good rubrics capture what matters.

Many features that define quality assessment at the state or district level are important at the classroom level, too. The difference is, the teacher has far more control over how writing is assessed in his or her classroom, where the components of assessment are an extension of the teacher's instructional style.

More teachers than ever before are sharing criteria openly with students—or even working with students to define together what it means to write well. I am closely associated with the six-trait model of writing, but I am not talking about using that model specifically. I am simply talking about clarifying what it is we value by putting it in writing and letting students and parents know how writing will be assessed. This is a must. If we think we can keep sound criteria in our heads and apply them consistently over time and across performances, we are kidding ourselves. We need the criteria in writing so we can look at them and say, "This is what I believe." As our thinking changes and we gain new insights about what makes writing work, we can revise our rubrics to reflect that thinking.

Countless rubrics and checklists for writing (and other areas of curriculum) are available now. But the *best* way to come up with a truly useful instructional rubric is to create it in partnership with students.

I have worked with rubrics for years, but have had remarkably little success encouraging teachers to develop their own versions. It is so much handier to take someone else's rubric off the shelf, especially if you like the way it's worded. I understand this—when you're tired or busy, the prepackaged dinner can look pretty good. But rubric (or checklist) development demands that we figure writing out, not take someone else's word for what works. The greatest value of a rubric or checklist lies not in the document itself, but in its development. Coming to grips with what we value in writing (or reading, math, or science) teaches us to understand the content area we are exploring and challenges our accepted beliefs.

Let's say you want your students to write strong descriptions. You might begin with a not-so-strong sample and ask them to identify what *doesn't* work:

> Charlie was an old dog with a difficult personality. He was sort of a dark color, and small as well. He didn't seem to like people. Charlie could not walk especially well and had trouble in cold weather. He had a very loud bark and a deep growl.

You might ask your students to respond to this piece, and to identify the salient features of problematic desccription:

- vague words: *old, dark, small, sort of, well, loud*
- lack of detail: *Charlie "had trouble." What sort of trouble?*
- undeveloped thoughts: *Charlie had a "difficult personality." How so?*
- missing information: *What breed of dog? How old exactly?*
- lack of support: *"He didn't seem to like people." How do we know this?*

Now you, or your students, could use this list to revise the original piece and create something stronger:

> Charlie was an eleven-year-old black miniature schnauzer. He had a perpetually frowning face, thick, bushy eyebrows tinged with gray, and a thickly muscled body shaved so close he always got the shivers in cold weather. He was blind in one eye, and perhaps that is what made him distrustful of almost everyone. Though his owner, Roberta, kept him on a fairly short leash, Charlie was stocky and

powerful for a dog only a foot high at the shoulder, and he would lunge for bikers' feet or ankles—even growling low in his throat as he slowly circled small children in their strollers. Arthritis in all four legs did little to improve Charlie's disposition. Though he would sink his few remaining teeth into any leg he could reach, it was hard not to feel sorry for him as he fought his way through snow or limped over the ice in cold weather.

In creating and reviewing this revision, you could identify with your students the features (call them traits or qualities if you like) of strong description:

- specifics: *eleven years old, arthritis in four legs*
- easy-to-picture-details: *black, bushy gray eyebrows, blind in one eye, foot high at the shoulder*
- shows rather than tells: *Instead of "Charlie didn't seem to like people" we get "Charlie would lunge for bikers' ankles."*
- information woven throughout the piece: *In the last line, we learn about the "few remaining teeth."*
- sensory details that go beyond the visual: *We hear Charlie growl, feel the cold of the snow and ice.*

Having agreed on what's important, you could turn this list of features for good descriptive writing into a checklist. And you could do the same for any genre. Best of all, it would have come from *you* and your students, not from any outside source. As an added bonus, you would now have a classroom checklist you could share with parents, who would see within the document precisely what their children are learning about good writing.

Checklists and rubrics are not complete until they are backed by samples of writing. Students have a right to see samples of what we want from them as writers. If we cannot produce them, we ought to take another look at our criteria to see if what we are asking of students is realistic.

Students need to see samples of a story that works versus a story that does not, a research piece with solid evidence and documentation versus one filled with generalities and unsupported claims. Think how helpful it might have been to *you* as a student writer if someone had said, "Here's an example of how to write a good persuasive essay, and let's talk as a group about what makes it work." Or, "Here's a sample of a persuasive essay gone astray—let's talk about some problems you can learn to avoid in your writing." Writers need to see both successful and less successful pieces. We learn as many lessons—perhaps more—from problematic writing as from strong writing. By analyzing and discussing such writing, students become teachers—of themselves and of one another.

Like those who participate in a large-scale assessment, students within the classroom have a right to be assessed by people who write themselves and who read, often and diversely. If we do not write ourselves, we may not respect time requirements for writing. Why should we? We're not the ones writing. We may not know whether our assignments are sensible, challenging, obscure in meaning, vague, confusing, enticing, too broad, too narrow, or of interest to anyone else. Nonwriters tend to focus on the surface features of writing, on things that are clearly observable; it takes a writer's eye to go deep inside writing, where ideas, voice, and organization work their magic. As George Hillocks tells us, "In the minds of some people, writing is one thing, but thinking is quite another. If they define writing as spelling, the production of sentences with random meanings, and punctuation, then they might have a case. But who would accept such a definition? Writing is the production of meaning. Writing *is* thinking" (NWP 2003, 198).

If we write ourselves, we understand the nature of writing. We know how hard it is to get the right personal slant on a topic. We know how hard it is to get going, when everything in our brains is searching for reasons and ways to procrastinate. We know that as writing unfolds, it moves in unexpected directions, inviting us down trails we didn't know we'd be exploring. We know that serious revision requires us to read our work aloud, more than once. When we write, we see in our own drafts the same problems we recognize in our students' writing: undeveloped ideas, erratic organization, miscue leads that fill a reader's head with expectations we as writers will never fulfill, tired language (we all reach for the jargon we know), stiff, pretentious, I'm-out-to-impress-you writing, and more. At the very least this is, or ought to be, humbling. At the very least, it ought to help us figure out what writers need—and therefore, what we ought to teach.

Assessors at the classroom level must be readers, too. It's the only way to develop an ear for what's good, what's musical, what's right. A practiced reader can spot good writing even when it's buried under messy handwriting or sloppy presentation. Her ear cuts right through all that. When a reader says, "I don't hear any voice in that writing, not a drop," it does not necessarily mean that no voice is there. Sometimes we forget that our assessment reflects ourselves as much as it does the performance we are assessing.

A city dweller who has never ventured into the forest may hear only silence—and may even say, "How do you *stand* the quiet? I need noise." This person's city ears haven't yet tuned in the pattern of smaller sounds: the scuttle of squirrel feet scrambling down the thick puzzle-like bark of an ancient Ponderosa pine, the soft thud of a deer's hoof landing on needle-cushioned earth, the barking of Canada geese about to hit the water, the buzz of hummingbirds motoring by like tiny feathered jets, and far in the distance, the disarmingly human wail of coyotes. By reading, we teach ourselves to listen for the layers of sound within each text. We teach ourselves to hear and feel the beat in a sentence like this one, so carefully crafted by Diane Ackerman:

> Imagine the brain, that shiny mound of being, that mouse-gray parliament of cells, that dream factory, that petit tyrant inside a ball of bone, that huddle of neurons calling all the plays, that little everywhere, that fickle pleasuredrome, that wrinkled wardrobe of selves stuffed into the skull like too many clothes into a gym bag. (2004, 3)

We assess writing as much with our ears as with our eyes. Ben Yagoda, author of *The Sound on the Page*, tells us that we read with our ears all the time, and that this comes from a long tradition of reading aloud or reciting words before print was commonly available, as well as from (for many of us) the sheer love of being read to:

> When we "get into" a book, the pleasant enveloping feeling brings us back to the childhood state of being read to by our parents. Bad writing keeps clearing its throat to wake us from our reverie. Psychologists report that all of us, whether or not we move our lips when we read, subvocalize, or silently recite the text to ourselves. (2004, 35)

Good classroom assessment goes beyond thoughtful evaluation, though. It's also passionate. Student writers have a right to a heartfelt response from us. Most teachers *do* respond passionately somewhere inside themselves; they just do not always let it out.

I recall working with a class of new teachers and sharing with them a piece of writing that made them laugh heartily. Everyone agreed it rang with voice. "What would you *say* to this writer?" I asked. There was silence. They were not sure what *words* would help this little writer know how strong her voice was. We are very accustomed to conveying our responses to writing in the form of grades or numbers. But these things are not what writers need, deep down. They need our voices, our hearts. They need to know their writing has touched us in some way.

This brings me to a second point about good commentary. It's not only passionate, but compassionate as well. There is a vast difference between honesty and rudeness. Ours is a society that thrives on rudeness. If you've watched a stand-up comedy routine lately, or been to the movies, or even tuned into a typical sitcom, then you know that smart remarks and belittling comments get laughs. Jaded views are considered sophisticated and chic. Tenderness, gentleness, and optimism are seen as hopelessly naive and childish. So-called reality television seems designed to teach us that only the ruthless survive, whether on jungle islands or stages, that morality is relative, and that abandoning cumbersome ethics is strategic. Is it? Why? Anyone can be a critic. Good teachers do something much harder: They look for the moment—the precise moment—at which a writer stumbles onto her true topic. They listen for that first whisper of the writer's voice, no matter how faint. They listen for the word or phrase too good to replace, for the rhythm of sentences that fall just right on the ear. A teacher's ear hears the deer in the forest.

We should remind ourselves too of the very real possibility that no matter how certain we feel about our responses, another evaluator might feel quite differently looking at the same piece of writing. No single assessment can ever be regarded as "the truth." As Peter Elbow reminds us, "One of the most trustworthy evaluations we can produce is a mixed bag: an evaluation made up of the verdicts or perceptions of two or more observers who may not agree" (1986, 223). Once we have this perspective, it helps us to not take ourselves too seriously, and to realize that assessment at its best offers support and insight, not judgment.

Just how fine-tuned are your own assessment skills? Look at the following pieces of writing, one a poem by a seventh-grade writer, one a short story from a second grader. In each case, imagine yourself sitting down for a chat with the writer. In each case, ask yourself, "What do I hear in this piece?" Listen for the layers of sound. Give yourself permission to respond with both compassion and passion.

The Andersons

Rachel Jordan Woods, Grade 2

Once there was a family. It was a nice family. The mother was Linda. The father was Bob. The boy was Jon. The girl was Marry Jo, and the baby was Laura.

They lived in a small apartment. One day, they decided to move. They packed their belongings. "Dad, where are we going to move?" asked Jon.

"To a farm."

"What is a farm?" asked Marry Jo.

"I don't know," said Dad.

One day, the Dad said, "I will go put the cow in the chicken coop and get some eggs."

Jon said, "I will go milk the pigs."

Marry Jo said, "I think I will go put the chickens in the pond."

Jon said, "I will go put the ducks in the pig pen."

Well, you know you can't do that, so they had a hard life.

Ode to Horses

By Laura Schweigert, Grade 7

I see you flash by
Wisps of
Cloud,
Earth and
Sky
Collide,
To make you,
My graceful friend.

On wobbly legs you stand,
Taking your first uneasy S
                          T
                           E
                            P
                             S,

As I watch you discover your world.
Like me,
You're an independent spirit,
You venture farther from your mother,
But she guides you back to safety within her reach.
You are a baby packed with dynamite,
And will grow into a strong young horse.

As we both grow,
We will earn each other's
Respect,
Trust, and
Guidance.

We must believe
One wrong step could prove fatal for one
Or both of us.

Each hoof beat must be
Steady,
Strong, and
Skilled.
Through an intense understanding,
We can communicate using
Mind,
Body, and
Spirit.
Performing for an audience—
Hearts will sing.
Hands will clap.
And dreams will come true.

Without you,
I would be
Lost,
Restless, and
Unsettled.
You have given me a future.

With you,
My friend,
I feel as if we could conquer the world.
My troubles are forgotten and,
I can see clearly again.
The horse will be part of me forever.

Student writers have a right to good personal assessment, too—self-assessment, that is. They have a right to assess their own work and to see and hear it differently from how we see and hear it. Their purpose is different. Whereas we assess to grade and to coach, they assess to understand and to revise. Our job is to help them do this well: to use sound criteria that they have helped develop, and to give each piece the interpretive reading it deserves, a reading designed to bring out each nuance of voice and fluency. Student writers will be skilled assessors if, like us, they are avid readers and practiced listeners. They will be skilled assessors if, like us, they write every day so that thinking like a writer becomes a habit. They will be skilled assessors if, like us, they continually think about what it is they value in writing.

As a teacher, you can do many things to help your students become more skilled at self-assessment. Create your own checklists with your students and revise them when you need to do so. Talk about literature not only as a body of ideas but as the work of writers. Each book, article, story, or essay has a lesson (or lessons) to teach us about writing well. Treat every piece of problematic writing as a lesson specially packaged just for you and your students, asking them, "If this were *your* piece, what would *you* do to make it stronger?"

Encourage students to revise their work by reading what they write aloud—more than once, if possible. Encourage them to think like readers, asking, "Does this make sense? Is this text pulling me in or pushing me away?" Such reading is essential to good self-assessment. Writer Susan Orlean emphasizes the importance of hearing her own text and imagining how a reader might respond:

> I read my pieces out loud when I'm writing, and if something doesn't sound like a natural sentence, I take it out. If something's too boring for me to read out loud, I take it out. If you find it too boring to read, just think how boring the reader's going to find it. (Yagoda 2004, 176)

As poet and essayist John Ciardi tells us, "The last act of writing must be to become one's own reader. It is . . . a schizophrenic process. To begin passionately, and to end critically, to begin hot and end cold; and, more important, to try to be passion-hot and critic-cold at the same time" (Brodie 1997, 82). This is where process and assessment (self-assessment, that is) come together. Writers hit a higher level of skill once they realize that revision is generative; revision takes us ever closer to our real meaning.

Writers are entitled to love their own work even when they stand alone in that judgment. We will know we've done a good job teaching our students to assess their work when they feel comfortable disagreeing with our judgments, and when they can support their disagreement so convincingly that we suspect they may be right. I don't mean that they should mindlessly embrace everything they create. None of us can afford to do that. Still, writers need backbone. They need the courage to believe in what they have written even when a critic or two fails to share their enthusiasm. After all, no one's work is loved by everyone. It simply isn't realistic. "Even the ancient mariner, with his wonderful tale, succeeded in stopping only one of three!" (Garfield in Brodie 1997, 105). Most students routinely play to an audience of one. It's always a gamble.

The most important things to know about writing cannot be represented by numbers. If you have ever caught your breath as you were reading, or closed your eyes to better envision the moment a writer was creating for you, or said to a friend, "Listen to this . . ." then you know what I mean. Yet, numbers have such power over us. We want to know the current GDP, the Dow average, the likelihood of rain, the average current life span, the number of carbs in an apple, a book's rank on the *New York Times* bestseller list, the number of steps we must walk each day to be deemed fit.

We are number obsessed, and in many cases, we attribute far too much importance to statistical information and not enough to the reality behind the numbers. We trust our calculators more than we trust our hearts. Albert Einstein once said that the most important things in the world could not be measured. So it is with writing. We cannot measure a child's confidence as a writer, her engagement in the writing process, the joy she feels when she creates something she feels proud of (regardless of what others may feel), her love of books, the sense of contentment she feels when someone reads aloud to her, the courage it takes for her to share her writing with another person, the satisfaction she feels in writing a note to a parent, or the profound admiration and gratitude she has for a writer whose words have transported her to another world. In the end, what matters most in the world of writing is immeasurable. So student writers have a right to assessment that is not just about numbers, but also includes room for a smile, a laugh, a sigh, applause, and the honest and passionate response that all writers hunger to hear.

An aside: In 1904, a horse called Clever Hans, who lived in Berlin, was thought for a time to be capable of doing mathematical calculations, including decimals and fractions. He would signal the correct answer to a problem by pawing the ground with his hoof the correct number of times. He shook his head to indicate zero. A clever psychologist determined, however, that Hans could not actually count. What he could do, it seemed, was to notice the most subtle raising of questioners' heads when they expected an answer—and an almost imperceptible relaxation of the body when Hans had reached the right number, and it was (apparently) time to stop. The idea that a horse might be capable of such perceptive interaction with humans was lost on people obsessed with measuring a far more superficial skill. As writer David Boyle notes, "Hans seems to have had an extraordinary intuitive intelligence, but because he could not actually do arithmetic, sadly, modern science lost interest" (Boyle & Roddick 2004, 32).

An Open Letter to an Assessor

SAMANTHA ABEEL

Don't tell me what I did wrong. Tell me what I did right. Just having the courage to put something on the blank surface before me is miraculous enough. To express something from my own inner thoughts—that in itself is an achievement. No matter how many times it takes, remind me of this accomplishment. Tell me everything I did well because my inner voice is critical enough. My inner voice is relentless, distorting things into negatives, always telling me I could do better, could do more. Soon it could become a voice saying, *Why bother anyway? I can't do this.* I need your encouragement to help me hear myself within the words.

Look for me in my writing. You will know if my written voice matches my outer voice. It's not about eloquence or beauty; it's about honesty. Did I push myself—not in comparison to others in the class, or in the field—but against *myself*? Does the meaning of my words hold true, regardless of how ugly or disjointed they may seem? Punctuation, grammar, different styles and forms of writing are all things that must be learned, and I need to know what changes are required for me to master them. But do not forget to look beyond such things to what is being said on the paper between your fingertips. Encourage me as a writer and thinker through exposure to the writing of others and through reading. Help me begin to pick out my *own* mistakes. Guide me to see and understand those things I have missed, but don't let me lose sight of what I have. Let what I have always be the starting point.

Writing is as simple as talking on paper. Never let me lose sight of that. As a baby, I did not learn how to talk by copying sentences into paper. I learned to talk by listening to the voices of my parents and others around me. What I heard became the foundation for the voice in my head. Long before I could write, or knew anything about the structure of a written sentence, I was talking in sentences. If I don't learn to write in the voice I speak with, before I am expected to apply the complexities of sentence structure, punctuation, and spelling, my writing will become the boring, arduous chore of mimicking the styles and forms of others. Finding and recognizing my inner voice later in life may be a challenge, but it is impossible to overstate its importance.

Fundamentally, writing or any creative endeavor needs to be nurtured and encouraged to happen, not expected . . . we have to be given the opportunity to do things badly before we can do things well. How our teachers choose to handle those fragile moments of exploration will either make or break the experience for us as writers. Meet me, the writer, where I am. Through positive feedback and reinforcement, be a trail guide for my path of discovery to powerful written self-expression.

SAMANTHA ABEEL, *who was diagnosed with a mathematical learning disability at age thirteen, is an accomplished writer who graduated with honors from Mount Holyoke College. She is the author of the ground-breaking and haunting ALA award-winning memoir* My Thirteenth Winter, *as well as the renowned* Reach for the Moon, *a book of poetry published when she was fifteen.* Reach for the Moon *won the 1994 Margot Markek Award, presented by the New York branch of the Orton Dyslexia Society in honor of the best book written on the subject of learning disabilities.* School Library Journal *said of it, "Every teacher of the gifted and the learning disabled needs to know about this book." Samantha, whose work has been featured on National Public Radio and in* USA Today, *currently makes her home in Traverse City, Michigan.*

Eight
The Right to Go Beyond Formula

My mother used to say that if you wanted to be a good cook, you had to like to eat. "I will not," she'd vow, "cook anything I wouldn't want to eat myself." That in a nutshell is a good philosophy for writing: We ought not to write anything we wouldn't want to read.

Sometimes—actually, almost *always*—good cooks tinker with recipes. Really good recipes are the result of previous tinkering to begin with. But then comes the need to make that vegetable soup your own, and so whimsically you leave out the bay leaf and add some fresh basil right off the windowsill. You omit the green beans no one likes and add a few of those red beans everyone loves. You angle the celery slices for more flavor, double the red onion the recipe calls for, throw in a splash of

In attempting to take the mystery away from writing and make it more accessible, the formulaic approach winds up hindering students from exploring their ideas, reactions, and interpretations—the rich chaotic mess from which true insight and thoughtfulness can emerge.

MARK WILEY
"The Popularity of Formulaic Writing"

red wine, and serve your version with jalapeño cornbread and a sprinkling of Parmesan. What's really great about this recipe is that *next* time you make this soup, it will be just a little different, depending on your mood. Cooking by the rules can never match cooking by inspiration. Of course, when guests ask you for the recipe, you have two choices: You can hand them an actual written recipe, which won't match at all the magical concoction they've fallen in love with, or you can say what my mother used to say, "Why don't you just watch me do it?" It took me years to realize she said this because she was making it up as she went along—every time.

Perhaps you're thinking that making soup is really quite different from writing, but actually they have a lot in common. Both can be done in a formulaic fashion, and when they are, the result fills you up while leaving you inexplicably hungry at the same time. In addition, formula leads to reassuring, sometimes maddening predictability. When you open a can of soup from the market, chances are you won't have any surprises. "Well," you might counter, "I wasn't looking for surprises, and really didn't want any, thank you very much." I'll buy that. We buy prepackaged food because it satisfies our need for calories in a convenient manner, and we trust it to be the same time after time . . . but is predictability something we're willing to settle for in our students' writing? When it comes to writing, surprise is not only something we should tolerate, but something we should seek out and treasure.

Formula, of course, is seductive. That's the thing. If it were obviously inferior, it would never have gained its current popularity. We like the idea of a thesis and three supporting points the same way we like "bed in a bag" linen. It's neat. It's tidy. It's packaged and labeled. We don't have to work very hard as readers, either, because everything is right where it's supposed to be, right when it's supposed to be there. We could cut formula writing apart and label the pieces, and later assemble an essay on any topic just by reaching for the right shelf. It's that organized.

This, of course, is not how thinking works. Thinkers are forever perceiving connections between things. Ask a thinker what a thimble symbolizes, and he will set to work making a hundred connections no one ever thought of before. Formula writers do not do this. They build the connections first, like Jell-O molds, then look for some information to fill in the blanks. This appears, at first, to work—that's the seductive part. We may not spot the weakness in the construction until we compare formula to real writing, and note the difference.

Let's say, for example, that I am writing a research article on pigs. I am going to begin with a thesis: *Pigs are amazing animals.* I will support this thesis with three paragraphs about pigs, each of them having a main point. I will flesh out my paragraphs by expanding the main point with one or two sentences, and providing an example to illustrate my point (another one or two sentences). In the last paragraph, I will conclude my essay with a summary statement about how intriguing pigs are. The skeleton of my essay, if I put it into outline form, would look something like this:

I. Thesis statement: Pigs are amazing animals.
   A. expansion of thesis
   B. quotation pertaining to thesis
II. Supporting statement 1: Pigs are friendly.
   A. expanding statement
   B. example relating to friendliness
III. Supporting statement 2: Pigs are diverse.
   A. expanding statement

B. example relating to diversity
IV. Supporting statement 3: Pigs are adaptable.
    A. expanding statement
    B. example relating to adaptability
V. Concluding paragraph
    A. summary of key points
    B. closing comment

When I write my essay using this outline, it will flow something like this:

> Pigs are amazing animals. They are among the most friendly, diverse, and adaptable animals in all the world. No wonder they play a part in so many civilizations. Author John Pukite has called them "truly great animals" (2002, 10).
>
> Pigs may be the friendliest animals on the farm. If you approach, they will usually run to greet you. Many people find their antics, including bathing in the mud and oinking loudly at visitors, quite entertaining.
>
> Pigs are also diverse. There are more than five hundred breeds of pig in the world. They range in size from more than two-thousand pounds to about twenty pounds. They also come in a wide range of colors, including blue.
>
> Pigs are adaptable. They can be found in cultures throughout the world. In many cultures, they are an important food source. In some parts of the world, feral pigs may live wherever there is shelter from the cold and a source of water.
>
> In conclusion, pigs have fascinated people for centuries. Some people keep them for pets while others look on them as a prime food source. Either way, pigs are among the most popular of domestic animals.

This is pretty dull stuff, but it's not entirely my fault. It is extremely difficult to go from formulaic prewriting and planning to interesting writing. That's one reason professional writers do not attempt it. The formula restrains the writer, like a leash. The writer thinks of something interesting to say, but feels the choke of the formula pulling her the other way. *Not now . . . don't say that . . . get back over here . . . that's better . . .*

In 1999, John Pukite, a native Minnesotan known for his quirky way of writing about domestic animals, composed an essay called "Why Pigs?" that became part of a book called *A Field Guide to Pigs* (2002). I bought Pukite's book in the Santa Fe airport bookstore, en route to a writing workshop. I was looking for something that would illustrate informational writing with flavor. I confess I had minimal interest in pigs until I opened Pukite's book. Every page held a bit of pig lore, most of which was in some way new to me, and all of which was expressed in a style best described as improvisational jazz—variations on a theme. Within moments, I found myself laughing aloud, and perusing the section on breeds, admiring the sleek lines of the Hampshire and noting that the Middle White looked very much like the pig of fairy tales. I also took a few moments to review the structure of Pukite's writing just to see how he had strung his thoughts together. There was no sign whatever of the five-paragraph essay, yet the book was easy to follow, informative, and entertaining. What was his secret?

Let's begin with that most imposing of all beginning points: the thesis. Which of these do you suppose is Pukite's thesis statement for the essay "Why Pigs?"?

1. Pigs oink. In a perfect world, this probably would be enough to appreciate pigs for all their wonders.
2. Pigs are the true entertainers of the farmyard.
3. Unappreciated though they are, pigs are truly great animals with lively personalities and a complete lack of manners.
4. Pigs are, lest we forget, the number one livestock animal for meat production in the world. (2002, 10)

This is one of those great quizzes where you cannot go wrong. No matter which response you picked, or even if you said *All of the above* or *None of the above*, you are right. Pukite had four key points to make and decided to make them all in one essay. He could have connected them with some banal umbrella statement like "Pigs are among the world's most fascinating creatures." Frankly, I'm glad he didn't. I can infer that for myself. The lesson of this piece is that you can have more than one thesis—or an overriding implicit thesis. And either approach will work.

Formulas for writing are based on the faulty premise that a piece of writing has only a few component parts—like plumbing. All we have to do is connect them in the right order, and everything works beautifully. Pukite's writing, by contrast, is a wonderfully woven tapestry of statistics, commentary, and imagery. But he uses each of these selectively—and at just the right moment. If he were following a statistic-commentary-image-statistic-commentary-image sort of rhythm, his writing would be as stiff and unyielding as an I-beam, as opposed to supple and accommodating.

In the opening passage, when Pukite is trying to convince us that pigs truly are wondrous characters, imagery dominates: Wander around any modern farm, he tells us, and you'll notice that "Cows are calm and meditative, chickens are frantic, and sheep are, true enough, sheepish." By contrast, "little

oinkers and porkers will come running to greet you with a hearty snort."
Catch them at sunrise "slurping and burping and slopping up the slop at the
trough" while little piglets "run around like bullets of muscle" (Pukite 2002,
10). I like this collage of pictures. The farm photo album. I won't get this
from directions that tell a writer "Main point, detail, detail; main point, detail,
detail."

Pukite's paragraph on variety is a study in organizational connections,
with one thought leading smoothly into the next. Here he takes a whole different tack, shifting from image-based writing to facts. We learn that there are five
hundred breeds of pigs, and that because of this number, there are wide variations in size and color. Size, in fact, may range from two thousand pounds—
"they are closely related to hippos after all"—to less than twenty pounds (for
a pet). Similarly, colors range from black, red, or blue to spotted or belted. What
makes Pukite so good is that he writes like a reader. A reader can only handle
so many images—or so many statistics. Then it's time to switch gears. A sen-
sitive writer knows when to make the shift. Something within his writer's mind
searches for balance: OK, I've given you multiple snapshots, so let me give you
some factual background, including the fact that there are one million feral pigs
in the United States and another sixty million on farms. And that last fact leads
right into Pukite's conclusion that pigs are "the number one livestock animal for
meat production in the world" (2002, 10).

One of my favorite nonfiction writers, Sneed B. Collard, has often commented that good nonfiction writing cannot merely pile up statistics like a log-
jam. "Writing needs to do a kind of dance," Collard says. "It can't be all facts.
You need to stir in some drama. Instead of a march, it might be more like a
tango—fact, fact, fact . . . dra-a-a-a-ma. See?" I do see.

Natural history writer David Quammen has mastered this step. In his
essay "Who Swims with the Tuna," Quammen (2001) begins with a factual
base, comparing the tuna to the dolphin:

> One of these animals breathes air. The other doesn't. One is a mam-
> mal, one isn't. . . . One is homoiothermic and one isn't. One seems
> to have an elaborate system of social behavior and one doesn't. One
> has performed altruistic and astonishing rescues of human swim-
> mers; the other is prized for sushi. (2001, 65)

This informational comparison, steady as a drumbeat, is climaxed by the juxta-
position of two hauntingly diverse dramatic moments.

> Entangled in a net, unable to swim backward, panicked, hampered
> from raising its blowhole clear of the water, a dolphin will drown. (65)

And second:

> Five or six quick strokes of the flukes and they are upon you, sleek, fast, graceful legions. They come a little larger than life, for water magnifies. They animate the void. With barrages of clicks and choruses of high-pitched whistling, with speed and hydrodynamic perfection, with curiosity, mission, agenda, and something like humor, they fill up the empty blue. (Brower 1989 in Quammen 2001, 67)

What formula told David Quammen that putting these two contrasting images together would give his writing more power than either could provide individually? What formula told him (three pages later) that instead of saying "The butchering of dolphins is a hard thing to watch," he should say, "The scene with the knife is hard to watch and tricky to contemplate" (70)? What follows is hard to read—for me at least. But by the time Quammen is punching home his personal argument, that "the death of six million dolphins in thirty years—as a by-product of purse-seining, merely to bring us cheap tuna with most of those six million carcasses dumped back into the ocean—has been unconscionably wasteful" (70), my stomach is in a knot and I have sworn off tuna forever.

Quammen asks whether his readers are "concerned with humanity's relationship with nature" or "merely concerned about Man's Special Friend at Sea, the dolphin" (67). I wanted to think that for me it was certainly the former, but Quammen's own accounts of brainy and empathetic dolphins seeking out the company of humans (no tuna do this) have made it the latter. So now I have suffered through graphic account of dolphins being filleted, only to have him remind me that his primary argument is not really about protecting dolphins at all—but about supporting "clear thinking about humanity's responsibility within the wider diversity of life" (71). Well, who can argue with that? What formula told Quammen to drive his main argument home at the end of the essay when his readers would be in a weakened emotional condition?

For anyone who doubts that formula limits rather than extends thinking, it's a good exercise to try to follow the trail through any well-written essay, drama, or story. How *does* one thought lead to another? For playwright Lynda Barry, the thoughts come so fast and hard that a whole chain of events is compacted into a single sentence in "Music Appreciation":

> Well one thing that they never tell you in the grade school is to enjoy singing while you can because eventually you are going to be divided up by who can sing and who can't sing, and the people who can sing will go to Choir, and the ones who can't sing won't sing, and may never sing again, and go to a class called "Music Appreciation"

where a teacher will give you a piece of cardboard printed with the life-size keys of a piano and then teach you how to play "Go Tell Aunt Rhody" on it to a record. (1998, 83)

What comes next? This is a question I love to ask students. Given what you've just read, given what you're thinking right now, given the questions and feelings in your mind, where do you think the writer will go? After all, writing takes readers on a journey. So when we play the part of the reader we should ask, *Am I enjoying the trip? Am I being led by the hand or left adrift on an open sea?*

If I am playing the formula game, it might occur to me that what's needed next are details about music appreciation, followed by details about choir. A sort of compare-contrast thing, with the advantages and disadvantages of each. It is almost impossible to grasp how unbearable this writing would be if it followed that path. But in thinking like a reader, Lynda Barry decides to take us to a dangerous place—the setting where it is decided who will go where. With this description, she puts us emotionally on edge, for we have all been there in one context or another. Who will be chosen? Who will be left behind with the cardboard piano? We are right there with her on the stage, waiting to be judged:

How you get tested for your singing is, the first week of junior high school you report to the auditorium during music period and find out you have to stand alone on the stage except for a ninth grader playing the piano, and sing "America the Beautiful" while the rest of the class sits around drawing on their folders or staring at you while they wait for their turns. You get a score and then that's it. The end. (84)

It's a rare person for whom this passage will not call up a memory. But you won't find these instructions in any formula: *Take the reader there. Make the reader feel it. Create tension. Detail, emotion, tension; detail, emotion, tension.*

I know the argument: formula is better than no organization at all. This is like saying that thinking in a confused way is better than not thinking at all. Is it? Formulaic writing will take our young writers to the upper limits of mediocrity, with pieces like the one I wrote on pigs earlier in this chapter. Such writing is easy enough to follow and makes sense on a simple level. It is devoid of complexity, passion, surprise, or art. It cannot make me see baby pigs as bullets or make me wonder why I care so much more about dolphins than tuna, or take me back to that junior high auditorium where one road led to glory and one to humiliation. So we must ask, are we teaching formula so that our students will be better writers—or so that we can read what they write effortlessly and quickly? Instant soup. "In my most cynical moments," says George Hillocks Jr., Professor of English at the University of Chicago, "I wonder if the master plan is to train people not to think. The logic of political speeches has much in common with the logic of the five-paragraph theme. If students learned to think and question, they might detect the nonsense in their representatives' speeches. Is that what the fear is? Is there a plan to keep students from thinking, a kind of subtle *1984*?" (2002, 204)

An imposed structure, even when it does not fit the content well, can make writing look stronger than it really is, particularly at first glance. This happens for a simple reason. Obvious structure (*first, second, third, last . . .*) is easy to spot, and encourages a momentary sense of relief in the reader: *Look . . . the connections are all made for me—I can just sit back and relax.* In truth, the mere presence of structural organizers tells us no more about writing than a house number tells us about the people living there. We need to open the door. Step inside. Stay for tea.

What we need to ask in analyzing a piece of writing is not whether the writer has identified three points, but whether *any* of the three points reflects research or sound thinking, whether they are relevant to or supportive of any main message, whether any of the points demonstrates original thinking, whether they are interconnected, and whether they are sufficiently well developed and presented to interest an attentive reader or teach the reader anything important. Counting is simple. Thinking is hard—hard to achieve and, consequently, hard to assess. Formula lets us off the hook.

Formula advocates argue that a structured approach is a way of helping writers who will not make it otherwise. I disagree. It can have the opposite effect. Struggling writers who follow a formulaic approach may seem to improve significantly at first, but in fact it is very hard for them to rise above a level we might call functional. That's because they can only go as far as the formula will take them, and formulas are, by definition, restrictive. Instead of lifting students up, as they purport to do, they effectively keep them in place.

A college friend once received this comment on her writing: "I think you have it in you to write competently, though not brilliantly." This is precisely what we say when we hand someone a formula. "Here," we tell them, "You poor struggling writer, you! Let me do the hard thinking for you—and you just fill in the blanks." This is presumptuous and condescending, but worse than that, it is wrong. Wrong because we are missing the whole point of teaching writing, which is not to crank out pieces of writing but to teach thinking. We must challenge our students to understand themselves and their world, not make connections for them. We must remain open, always, to the possibility that students are capable of thinking at a much deeper level than their initial attempts at writing would indicate. And we must remember that formulas, drills, and fill-in-the-blank exercises have one important feature in common: They are deadly dull. If we want to ensure that students have no interest in writing and avoid it whenever possible, then we have only to make it tedious, repetitious, and unimaginative. They will get the idea.

If we let go of formula, though, what then do we teach instead? What do we tell our student writers that they can cling to? First, write to create reading. Everything, however tiny, that you struggle with as a reader, from faulty punctuation to disjointed organization, is a problem for you to solve as a writer. Learn what to do by reading. Take what is hard and make it easy for someone else.

Second, read as you go. Read everything, every word you write, aloud. Listen. Keep asking, does this make sense? What questions have I raised in the reader's mind? What feelings have I brought out? Where do I take the reader next?

Third, think of writing as a journey. It has a destination, yes. That is the main idea. The force behind the writing. But look at any map and you will see that, with few exceptions, there are many paths to take you from A to B. The road you choose as a writer determines not only how long your journey will be, but also how interesting. Some side trips are allowed, but they cannot be too long or wander too far or you find yourself on a different journey altogether.

Fourth, think about what terms like *expand, support,* or *detail* really mean. How do you expand or support an idea? Sometimes you tell a story, or quote someone who agrees but who puts things in such an interesting way that you want his or her voice to flavor your writing. Sometimes, you include a fact—that a pig can weigh two thousand pounds, for instance. And maybe you help the reader to digest that fact by noting that the pig is a distant cousin of the hippo.

Detail is any information that helps a reader get a grip on an idea. If you write in generalities—*He is an unffriendly and untidy person*—your readers will feel as if they are free falling, with nothing to hang onto. But if you feed them sensory impressions, as author Lynda Barry does in describing Mr. Madsen, the music teacher, you give them a front-row seat with a close-up view of the world as you see it: "He has tiny, light yellow teeth and his hair is cut so you can see right through to the white skin on his head. And no matter what you are doing, he always looks at you like you are giving him the biggest headache" (1998, 86).

Finally, look at what professional writers do. See if you can trace the path of their thinking, as in this example. In *The Medusa and the Snail,* Lewis Thomas gives us a lesson on punctuation that is also a lesson on how to think like a reader *as you write.* Let me show you by placing Thomas's words on the right, and my interpretation of how his thinking took him there on the left:

Let me show you.

Want to know what it's like?

So don't we need exclamation points?

And if it doesn't?

Exclamation points are the most irritating of all.

Look! They say, look at what I just said! How amazing is my thought!

It's like being forced to watch someone else's small child jumping up and down crazily in the center of the living room shouting to attract attention.

If a sentence really has something of importance to say, it doesn't need a mark to point it out.

And if it is really, after all, a banal sentence needing more zing, the exclamation point simply emphasizes its banality! (1995, 127)

When we take time to track the thought processes of our best writers, a useful thing for students to do, we discover that while they do not rely on formula, they do rely on something that is worth teaching, namely, the keen anticipation of a reader's needs. In *Because Writing Matters*, the National Writing Project (NWP) authors remind us that "Doing it well means being both a writer and reader" (2003, 9). Writers must live on both sides of the text, wearing two hats all the time. This is a delicate balancing act that takes practice, vision, and continual inner dialogue about the journey toward meaning. That's why it is so important for writers to write—and to read—every day.

Formula writing takes away both the pain and the reward of thinking like a reader. Formula says, "Do this, and the reader will understand you." Perhaps. But learning to think like a reader is essential to writing skill. So while a formulaic approach may guide me through one piece of writing, it cannot necessarily help me with the next one, where audience and purpose are different. The NWP authors quote evaluators Charles Cooper and Lee Odell to emphasize the point that student writers need a wide array of strategies for dealing with the hundreds of diverse writing tasks that await them: "It may be that, ultimately, we value some general qualities, such as 'organization' or 'quality of ideas.' But we now know that the strategies that make good organization in a personal narrative may differ from the strategies that make a good report of information or a good persuasive letter" (2003, 15).

One set of strategies will not fit all writing occasions. A set of directions to guide me from Albuquerque to Santa Fe will be of no help to me tomorrow when I travel on to St. George. We cannot possibly create enough formulas to fit every situation. Nor should we. The very presentation of a formula or outline suggests a belief that writing is simple and reductive, when we ought to be teaching just the opposite. We ought to tell students the truth: that writing is complex, and that every single writing situation is different, and must be thought through as carefully and sensitively as a conversation with someone one has never met but would like to have for a friend.

Formula has other pitfalls as well. For one thing, it discourages independence. A formula is a crutch, after all, and providing people with crutches makes them fearful of new situations. Writing is *all* about new situations. A new purpose, new audience, new information, and new ways of presenting it. The problem with the formula is that it puts the emphasis on the wrong place: the writing. Start with a main idea, add three supporting details, close with an observation, and you have an informational piece. Add to this recipe an opposing viewpoint and a counter argument and you have a persuasive argument.

What we ought to focus on is the *writer*. Being a good informational writer takes more than a main idea and three supporting points. It takes a questioning mind, a capacity for curiosity. It also takes an understanding of what research is really about: the ability to formulate questions that matter and to imagine where one might find the answers to those questions. The place to begin teaching informational writing is not with a statement—*Here's your formula*—but with a question: *What are you curious about?*

Students are interesting people with interesting things to say. "Tell me one true thing," we ought to say. "What's important? What do you think I ought to know? What should I care about?" Then of course we have to do our part; we have to be genuinely interested in their response.

Writers are also people who see what others miss. William Faulkner once said, "Writing is one-third imagination, one-third experience, and one-third observation" (Brodie 1997, 1). Observation is mostly habit, and you can do much to encourage it. Bring an aquarium with one goldfish into your classroom and ask students to write about it for half an hour. Let their thoughts carry them along—to wherever. Each student will see something different, and that's the point. Under no circumstances should you assess the writing they do. This is only a warm-up. It's practice in thinking like a writer. The way we look at a goldfish when we take time to *really* look, to notice its markings, its way of moving, its way of being, to consider what it reminds us of—that is the way a writer must look at *everything*: a friend, a boss, a parent or sibling, a lover, a teacher, a stranger, a child, his own reflection in the mirror—or a mark of punctuation.

Being yourself. Telling the truth. Taking a close look. Those are the things a writer cannot survive without. Technique is just frosting on the cake. We make a mistake when we begin with technique. We need to begin with our students, who they are, what they feel. Writing lives inside us. Picture-book writer Maurice Sendak describes it this way: "I feel it in me like a woman having a baby, all that life churning on inside me. I feel it every day: it moves, stretches, yawns. It's getting ready to get born. It knows exactly what it is" (Brodie 1997, 34). The secret to good writing instruction is not in a formula. It's in your students' eyes.

The most important reason to avoid formula—indeed, to run from it as fast as our feet will carry us—is that it stifles thinking. Hillocks alleges that formula not only fails to "support higher level thinking skills" but actually imposes "a way of thinking that eliminates the need for critical thought." He goes on to explain that one widely accepted example of formulaic writing, the five-paragraph theme, has been banished at many universities because it is seen as inappropriate, simplistic, and superficial (2002, 136). It is easy to understand why university professors would feel this way if we think about it. Students who follow a formula or prescribed outline may not take time to assess the value or authenticity of the information they use to fill in the blanks. Does it make sense? Does it really expand or authenticate or validate the point it is intended to support? Is it relevant or critical to the reader's understanding? What does it matter, so long as all the blanks are filled? Directed writing, like painting by numbers, requires no vision of the whole, no sense of a writer's journey in finding, developing, and refining an idea. Formulaic writing encourages vacuous thinking and freedom from personal investment. In short, it undermines the very soul of what we seek to accomplish through writing instruction.

Charles Wysocki, the beloved folk artist, begins his remarkable portfolio titled *Heartland* with these words:

> There is a country in my mind, a landscape in my heart, a place that does not appear on any map but is so clear and sharply detailed that to paint it, I have only to look within. It is a place of wonder and surprise, instantly familiar to all who view it with the eyes of a curious child. It is where things make sense and love holds. It is the past as it ought to have been. (1994, 13)

The landscape of the heart cannot appear on a map because it belongs to the artist. It is that individual landscape with its unique features, a vision unlike any other, that we want our student writers to share. You alone, we must tell them, have this landscape in your heart, this country in your mind. I trust you to share it through your own words and in your own way. I cannot settle for less.

No Training Wheels

STEPHEN KRAMER

No training wheels. No steadying hand on the seat. No one to catch you if you fall.

Every time I begin a new piece of writing, I'm reminded of what it's like to ride a bicycle for the first time. Uncertainty about what to do and when to do it. Worries about crashing. And the nagging feeling that, perhaps, this task is far too complicated to have any chance of success.

I have written a great many stories and I still don't know how to go about it except to write it and take my chances.

—JOHN STEINBECK

Of course, if the writing goes well, those feelings eventually give way to the satisfaction of completing the task. If the writing goes *really* well, the feelings give way to the wonder, exhilaration, and mystery of the creative process.

But I haven't yet found any shortcut through the beginning stages of writing. There are so many possibilities, so many trails leading in different directions. The only way to make any headway is to start trying them out. The map has to be constructed from scratch every time.

In the best writing—writing that makes you want to grab whoever's nearby and say, "Here, read this!"—the trails lead to unexpected and delightful places. Voice, ideas, and organization work together in ways that are peculiar to the writer and to the topic. Information and presentation combine in ways that couldn't possibly be predicted by any formula. The writing sings, and the reader senses that this is just the way the story needs to be told.

How do we help children achieve this kind of writing? I think we begin by reading aloud to them, often, pointing out passages that speak to us. We share and evaluate samples of writing with children, helping them develop the ability to look at their own writing critically. We model writing for children so they'll understand the decisions that writers face, word after word, sentence after sentence, paragraph after paragraph. We encourage young writers, acknowledging that writing is almost never easy. But most importantly, I believe that we give young writers much freedom and support in making their own choices in their writing. How else will they be able to figure out how their stories should be told?

As an elementary teacher working at a time when more and more attention is focused on high-stakes tests, I've thought often about the relationship between assessment and writing instruction. At its best, writing assessment helps young writers and their teachers communicate with each other about what makes writing good. Such assessment opens young eyes to different writing styles and prompts discussions about why some of us like one kind of writing and others like another.

But writing assessment can also have negative effects. When test pressures drive classroom practices, writing instruction can quickly become formulaic, with emphasis on schemes designed to increase test scores. I've watched creative students attempt to force their ideas into multiple paragraphs with identical topic sentence–supporting details–concluding sentence construction. I know of teachers who have taught their students to cram sentences full of adjectives and to sprinkle similes indiscriminately through paragraphs in the belief that this practice will help students score higher on writing tests. I wonder, though, whether anyone has calculated the effects of writing test pressures on students' love of writing.

We do need to help our students understand and apply concepts—like topic sentences, supporting details, and concluding sentences—creatively and appropriately. We do need to help our students learn to use adjectives and similes correctly—and sparingly. But when I read student work that's filled with cookie-cutter paragraphs or sentences strangled by adjectives, I always have a sense of regret and a bit of an ache. I'm left wondering how those writers would have surprised and delighted me had they been encouraged to choose their own paths and tell the stories in their own authentic voices.

Kurt Vonnegut has this to say about writing: "We have to continually be jumping off cliffs and developing our wings on the way down." Those of us who work with young writers need to be sure we keep our focus on the creative heart of writing. We need to give our young writers courage and faith. With courage they'll be willing to jump off the cliff, to take risks, experiment, and try fresh approaches in their work. With faith, they'll have confidence that they'll find their wings—and keep searching until they discover just how their stories should be told.

Stephen Kramer *is the author of* Hidden Worlds, Eye of the Storm, How to Think Like a Scientist, *and other books for young readers, all rich with imagery and voice. He teaches fourth grade at Hockinson Intermediate School in Brush Prairie, Washington, where he enjoys sharing his writing (both finished and in process) with his students. Steve is currently working on a book about scientific cosmology and religious thought, while simultaneously learning to play the uilleann bagpipes.*

Nine

The Right to Find Your Own Voice

Voice is the human spirit. It is the essence of self. It calls to us from the page and says, "Listen to me. This is who I am."

Voice not only drives the writing; it is, beyond the simple sharing of information, the very reason for writing. Voice comes from *who we are*, from the deepest part of ourselves, from the most sacred beliefs that define us. Like a river rising from the earth, voice carves a path through the thickest underbrush of verbiage, shaping the landscape around it, and retreating only when the source—the self—runs dry.

I wish we could change the world by creating powerful writers for forever instead of just indifferent writers for school.

—MEM FOX
Radical Reflections

Only one sort of writing can afford to go voiceless, and that is the sort in which a technical writer speaks to a technical reader—as in a medical treatise on the inherent risks of performing appendectomies. In such writing, the writer deliberately, carefully removes him- or herself, getting out of the way so the message can have center stage and consume the reader's full attention. Writing that plays to our emotions is out of place in such a context; we need to get on with the operation. Good technical writing is sleek as polished steel. It is the essence of message, from which all fingerprints have been wiped clean.

It's important to keep in mind that we read technical books because we need the information. We need to know what's in the operating manual, the tax code, a legal contract, or fire safety regulations. Voice is a nonessential in such writing, and may even be perceived as an intrusion, because there is no need for the writer to reach out to the reader. What the reader is after is information *only*, and voice can be a distraction.

At other moments, though, we read not because we have to, but because something within the text speaks to us. In the hands of a thoughtful and passionate writer, voice becomes not only an extension of self, but a tool for capturing and holding the reader's attention. Teacher and writer Bruce Ballenger calls writing a way of extending a conversation about a topic, a conversation enhanced by voice (2004, 15).

Voice is highly individual. Among professional writers whose voices are finely honed, this is immediately recognizable. Here are three voices you might know:

> *Voice 1*
> The mind travels faster than the pen; consequently, writing becomes a question of learning to make occasional wing shots, bringing down a bird of thought as it flashes by. A writer is a gunner, sometimes waiting in his blind for something to come in, sometimes roaming the countryside hoping to scare something up.

> *Voice 2*
> We are fighting to save a great and precious form of government for ourselves and for the world.

> *Voice 3*
> I hate the waiting room because it's called the waiting room so there's no chance of not waiting. It's built, designed, and intended for waiting. Why would they take you right away when they've got this room all set up?

Any immediate guesses? Suppose I tell you that one of them is E. B. White from the classic *The Elements of Style* (Strunk & White 1979, 69). You can pick that out quite easily now, can't you? One of them is, as you may have guessed, Jerry Seinfeld (from *SeinLanguage* [1993, 94]), whose voice is so distinctive that people from age eight to eighty identify it almost at once. The remaining voice is the one you are probably least likely to nail without a hint, though it would not, I think, be confused with the others. It is Franklin Delano Roosevelt (Brallier and Chabert 1996, 171). Now the matching becomes easy.

Suppose I tried to confuse you, though. If I were to tell you that the top voice belonged to Seinfeld, your reader's ear would respond, "No way! It's too metaphorical, too elegant, too formal, too poetic by far." Voices have features, textures, and no two are exactly alike. Similarly, if someone told you that the third voice belonged to Roosevelt, that reader's ear would counter, "Don't be ridiculous. That is a humorous, flippant, and irreverent voice. It's not presidential—and it's definitely not Roosevelt." Exactly.

Some student voices are this readily identifiable, but usually such distinctive individuality is a quality that develops over time. It goes hand in hand with sense of self, and matures in the same way. In a young writer's work, we often get a hint of the mature writer to come. As a fifth grader, Nikki wrote the following entry in her portfolio, describing her project on Paraguay:

> The most important thing I learned was about the vast diversity of people living in South America. At the end, we had a big fiesta in the gym and everybody displayed his or her project. We had music going all the time, and we dressed in Latin American clothing and danced. I loved it. I think I did a pretty good job on my project considering that compared to the guy that got Brazil, the library had squat on my country. Same with the bookstore. They had about 10–15 books on Brazil, but I could only find one that worked for me. Apparently no one visits Paraguay. How come? They should. Joel actually wanted Paraguay, but that was only because his sister had it two years ago.

We hear a combination of energy and honesty, both good ingredients for voice. Who is this writer going to be? Someone, we might predict, who will write with confidence—and a touch of humor.

As a high school student, Nikki wrote a research piece on method acting, which opens this way:

> The year is 1880. The theater is dark, except for one figure, illuminated on the stage. The figure, Prince Hamlet, begins his famous soliloquy. . . . The delivery of the lines is perfect, each word enunciated, clear from the rest. However, in the actor's face, there is no indication he feels the pain behind the words. While the character of Hamlet is clearly faced with a difficult decision—*To be or not to be*—the actor is only thinking what he might make for dinner—*To shop or not to shop*. The playgoers scan the face and find, in place of intensity, a sort of placid detachment. Wherever this person's mind and heart and center of grief reside, they are not at home right now. The audience does not believe this actor is Hamlet. And the reason they do not believe it is because the actor does not believe it himself.

This a more controlled voice. It reflects a flair for dramatic presentation of ideas, and an adult awareness and perspective, along with the rhythms that make a voice distinctive and recognizable. Read it aloud (you can be sure this writer did) and you will see that it flows easily, gracefully, phrase to phrase, line to line. And while the humor has grown more subtle and more deliberate, this piece still echoes that cut-to-the-chase voice from a few years ago.

Like our speaking voices, our writing voices vary not only with time, but also with the situation. We use a slightly different speaking voice when whispering to a lover, calming an unfriendly dog, seeking a loan, addressing the crowd at a daughter's wedding, berating a rude driver, or cheering on the football team. Similarly, a writing voice may be adamant, apprehensive, pedantic, sarcastic, or wistful. It may be dressed to the nines or lounging in sweats. Our friends always recognize us, no matter how we are attired. Similarly, no matter how dressed up or laid back the text, there is always something of the writer behind the words. "Writers I've loved," says author Susan Orlean, "I always felt I could tell you exactly what they're like, even if we've never met and they don't even write that much in first person, because there's some sense of being that kind of permeates the stories" (Yagoda 2004, 174).

It is a common misconception that voice is an afterthought, like salad dressing on the side. When we write from deep inside ourselves, voice emerges as naturally as the expression on a surprised, enraged, dismayed, or enamored face—unless we deliberately repress it. Voice can be controlled, but when we try to conjure it up, the result becomes self-conscious and artificial: "I *am* enraged, Herman. *Really*. This is how I *look* enraged." When we write what we know, and when we feel passionate about the message, the voice literally boils over.

This is why, in teaching voice, we cannot just say, "Sean? Could you think about adding some more voice right here?" When we understand where voice comes from, our focus is on what *precedes* voice, and gives rise to voice, namely the writer's passion, knowledge, and sense of conviction. Then our questions go right to the heart of the matter: *Sean, let's talk about the research you did for this piece. I'm sensing that some additional information could help. OR, Just at this moment—are you saying what you really think and feel, or imagining what someone else might wish to hear? What is the most important thing you want to say? And what do you want me to believe or feel or think as I read this?*

When a writer knows her topic inside and out, and believes in the message right down to her toes, there is no stopping the voice. In a state writing assessment a few years ago, a middle-school writer expressed his weariness with the emphasis on voice in classroom instruction. At that time, teachers often used the phrase "writing from the heart" to represent the kind of honesty and openness we called voice. In what turned out to be a stellar example of irony, the student commented in his essay, "Give writing from the heart the boot . . . I'm sick and tired and fed up with it." In reading this, one teacher remarked, "That's exactly what we're looking for, isn't it?" Yes, that's writing from the heart.

Voice also comes from perspective. What do you see when you look at a spider? Arachnid? Nuisance? Monster? Good luck symbol? Hunter? Biology project? Or something else . . . :

Creepy Spider

Creepy spider
plotting
a poisonous path
up the long trunk—
Weren't you a widow
in a previous life?
A husband lost . . .
A little black body gained . . .
Bitter to the core . . .
Looking with eight eyes
filled with scorn.
Only living to
die another day.

When we say that voice comes partly from perspective, that is another way of saying that voice works in harmony with ideas to create a larger message. The words "a little black body gained" are not meant only to create an image, but to convey an implicit reproach: "Look how little you gained for your sacrifice." As Donald Murray says, "Voice can also tell the writer what the subject is. The way we write about the subject tells us how we think and feel about it, what is important to us and what is less important" (2004, 22). No wonder that, in writing our way *onto* our real topics, we find our voices as well.

Many people think that formality, or objectivity, is the opposite of voice. Not really. A reserved tone often signals that voice is in hiding—or is being held in check in order to let attention fall on the message. In fact, the opposite of voice is indifference—the most insidious enemy of good writing. Indifference says to a reader, "This is a dull topic about which I have not one shred of curiosity. But if you do, read on. I'm sure I don't care." Indifference leaves us feeling we've been left outside, standing in the rain, with no hat and no one to notice. Strong voice, by contrast, shows awareness of the world, interest in the topic, and concern for the reader. It touches us like the kindness of someone opening an umbrella as we step out the door. It says, "Hey—have you got a minute? I've got something fascinating to tell you—and I want to make sure you get it." For example, my printer, like most, came with a service manual. It has this message in bold:

> By the time you get around to calling for service, you may be pulling your hair out in frustration. However, the quality of the information you give us will have a direct impact on how quickly we can get you back up and running. Relax. (Hewlett Packard, 2002, 7)

I like this message. It's comforting. It sounds as if it were written by someone who has actually had printer problems, and it makes me believe a real human will be on the other end of the phone if I need to call. I won't be left out in the rain.

Why is it so important to encourage voice? First, because voice is what makes us human, individual, unique. Voice shows itself in our writing, and is found in every way we express ourselves, through art and dance, the way we walk or use our hands, the way we laugh or sing or cry, the expressions we use to convey our emotions, the way we touch a flower or hold a child or kiss someone we love. Voice is the self, in all its guises, in all its variations. When we celebrate voice, we celebrate the individual.

Second, voice is power. Power to make readers listen. To make them remember, to alter their beliefs, to make them feel something they did not feel a second ago. Writing that has voice can make a difference. When we encourage voice, we say to students, "I want you to write things that matter. Things people will read and remember. I want your words to be heard."

The issue of whether voice can be taught is controversial. Some would argue that voice is a gift. You have it or not. But I would counter, "When is this not true in education?" Is there *anything*—spelling, fractions, penmanship, calculus, physics, drawing, driving, tumbling, football, keyboarding, music—about which we can honestly say, "We all have equal talent and will all learn this equally well"? So then, why not coach each writer to the highest level he or she can attain? All writers have voice. Not all writers know it, though. As a result, not all writers express their voice. Sometimes this is because they are afraid it will not be well received, or they simply do not believe the voice is in there. We must help them believe.

It's also said that voice is like personality. We cannot teach people to have personality—can we? Not directly, perhaps. We probably cannot *directly* teach honesty, individuality, or commitment to a topic, either. But we can point out the importance of such things, illustrate them in the writing of others, make it clear how much we value them, watch for them in our students, model them in our own writing, and comment on them—diligently—each time they occur. What we notice, approve, and openly appreciate we're likely to see more of.

Our verbal and written comments, expressions, and reactions provide more encouragement than we know. They help young writers feel sure of their footsteps on their way to finding a voice that is theirs alone.

We can also open our students' ears to a wide range of voices, and as we do so, we discover, along with our students, that voice is addictive. Once we begin reading books that resound with voice, we can scarcely bear to read the ones that don't. Once we begin listening for voice, we never read anything—even our own work—the same way again.

On the way to finding their own voice, our students may try on some other voices, imitating the writers they admire most. This can be a very useful thing to do. Imitation is demanding, for one thing. Students must pay very close attention if they are truly to sound anything like, say, Sandra Cisneros or Dave Barry. They have to capture the rhythm, the flavor, the punctuation style, the preferred vocabulary, even the attitude. Moreover, moving from one voice to another helps students develop extraordinary verbal flexibility. It's a long stretch from Cisneros to Barry—or Hemingway to Seinfeld. Stephen King recalls very clearly experimenting with various voices:

> When I read Ray Bradbury as a kid, I wrote like Ray Bradbury—everything green and wondrous and seen through a lens smeared with the grease of nostalgia. When I read James M. Cain, everything I wrote came out clipped and stripped and hard-boiled. When I read Lovecraft, my prose became luxurious and Byzantine. I wrote stories in my teenage years where all these styles merged, creating a kind of hilarious stew. (2000, 147)

Students need to read (and hear) a wide range of literature in order to understand what creates—or hinders—voice. As we read, we need to pause and point out, or let students discover for themselves, those qualities that affect voice most. Generalizations, for example, are toxic, whereas detail gives text vitality. In the emotional "Fourteen Turns," a story from *Nerves Out Loud*, Carellin Brooks might have written, *Olivia was a shoplifter. She was pretty good at it, too.* But such generalization would cheat us, the readers, out of every moment that is important to the story, and would also ensure that we cared not one whit about what happened to Olivia. Instead, Brooks puts us right at the scene of the crime, so we can watch Olivia in action, marvel at her bravado and skill (even if we disapprove of shoplifting), and wonder, along with her friends, whether she'll get by with it:

> My friend Liz—Olivia, she liked to be called, on a lark—was a good shoplifter, maybe the best among us. She drifted around the 7-11

next to our school, singing to herself and flinging big-ticket items—chocolate bars, baked goods, ice cream—into the cavernous depths of her black shoulder bag, while we, her more nervous friends, grouped ourselves near the three-for-a-dollar hot-dog cooker and eyed the oblivious counter boy. (Musgrave 2001, 34)

Olivia "drifting," the "nervous friends" sticking close to the hot-dog cooker, the "cavernous depths" of Olivia's bag: these details contribute to mood as well as the visual effectiveness of this sketch. This is a happening, an adventure, a ground-breaking initiation. The details and the words—like "cavernous depths"—make it so.

Of course, pointing this out is one thing. Details cannot be spooned onto writing, like M&M's® onto ice cream. If students are to write with detail, they must first *read for detail* so they know what they are striving for. They must identify the details themselves, underline or highlight them, and talk about them. Then, they must develop a writer's habit of looking closely at the world, reading it much the way we read books, and not resting till they, like Brooks, find the precise word to reflect what they see, the only word that will do—not the *shy* counter boy, the *quiet* counter boy, or the *disinterested* counter boy . . . but the *oblivious* counter boy.

Writer Flannery Conner says, "I know a good many fiction writers who paint, not because they're any good at painting, but because it helps their writing. It forces them to look at things" (Brodie 1997, 41). To look closely and to discover what others might miss is the foundation of all good writing. Writers are detail obsessed. They never stop noticing, never stop writing—in their minds. This obsession is what we need to teach.

What else affects voice? Verbs. Verbs and precise nouns support writing; adjectives and adverbs weight it down. In *"Come on, rain!"* Karen Hesse finds simple but just-right verbs to set up an atmosphere of apprehension and hope among people coping with drought: "Up and down the block, cats pant, heat wavers off tar patches in the broiling alleyway. Miz Grace and Miz Vera bend, tending beds of drooping lupines." Moments later, Tessie sees the "gray clouds, bunched and bulging under a purple sky" and whispers to us, "A creeper of hope circles 'round my bones" (1999).

Panting, wavering, bending, tending, drooping, bunching, bulging, and *circling*—these words give motion, grace, and a kind of internal rhythm and pulse to the writing. How different it would have been had Hesse kept the cats and people and vines motionless: *The cats felt hot. The tar was really hot. Grace and Vera were in their flower garden. Some gray clouds were in the sky. I hoped it would rain.* Strong verbs turn still-life into video. And when Hesse writes "creeper of hope," we have a noun (*creeper*) posing as a verb and almost getting by with it.

We must encourage students to make their writing move, too. They need to abandon excessive adjectives and adverbs, and call on lean verbs to carry the weight. In Hesse's description, the cats don't breathe heavily. They *pant*. The heat doesn't rise in shimmering waves from the pavement. It *wavers*. Clouds don't move in the sky. They *bunch* and *bulge*. Verbs are the fuel that makes writing go.

Dialogue matters because when characters speak, they take on style and attitude. They develop character. They become open and vulnerable because we see what makes them tick, what motivates them. In order for these things to happen, though, they need to sound believable. Consider this interchange:

"Hello," said Bill.

"Hello," said Riley. "What is your name?"

"I am Bill," said Bill. "Do you want to have some fun?"

"Oh, yes," said Riley.

Many beginning writers (and some novelists) create dialogue just like this because they have not taken time to listen to people speak, or to capture the irregularities, the rhythms, the give-and-take that marks genuine conversation. By contrast, anyone who has read a Frog and Toad book by Arnold Lobel knows the power of authentic dialogue to generate voice. Lobel's genius is that he writes at a level young readers can understand readily, yet creates complex characters to whom adults can relate:

> "You have been asleep since November," said Frog.
>
> "Well then," said Toad, "a little more sleep will not hurt me. Come back again and wake me up at about half past May. Good night, Frog." (1970)

Voice is also about rhythm. It cannot be fully appreciated with the eyes alone. It cries to be heard. Voice is the rhythm of Sandra Cisneros telling us, "Some day I will have a best friend all my own. One I can tell my secrets to. One who will understand my jokes without my having to explain them. Until then I am a red balloon, a balloon tied to an anchor" (1989, 9). That's a beat that cannot be denied. "Don't repeat words," we tell our students. We ought to tell them, "Don't repeat unless you can do it like Cisneros—then, for God's sake, don't let anyone stop you."

We teach and encourage voice when we read aloud without inhibition or hesitation, with all the passion we can muster. In doing so, we are modeling for our students precisely what we want them to do *with their own text*. If they read without inflection, punctuation will look arbitrary, meaning will be linked to a literal decoding of words instead of an interpretive projection of message, and voice will seem an elusive, abstract concept, not something that grabs you with both hands and commands attention. Reading with passion and writing with voice are flip sides of one coin.

Your ear will tell you—always—where the voice lies. Read these five sentences aloud, and let your writer's ear tell you which one sounds best:

1. The old woman flung off her cape and leaped onto the stage, and she moved like a cat when she did it.
2. The old woman moved like a cat when she flung off her cape and leaped onto the stage.
3. When she leaped onto the stage, flinging off her cape, the old woman was moving like a cat.
4. Moving like a cat, the old woman flung off her cape and leaped onto the stage.
5. The old woman flung off her cape and like a cat, leaped onto the stage.

Students need to do this very thing. They need to read aloud, to compare, to try a single sentence three, four, or even five different ways, and to make choices. Poet Billy Collins says that "Eighty percent of revision is rhythmical—making changes to make the right music" (Yagoda 2004, 145). Author Bebe Moore Campbell echoes this thought, telling us, "I always employ music in all my books. I'm always looking for a rhythm, looking for a click in my head" (Yagoda 2004, 43). When we teach students to read aloud, we teach them to rely on their ears as they write and as they revise—to listen for the "click" in their heads, and to know when the notes and the rhythm are making the writing dance. Though there is no "right" answer to my question about the five sentences, I like the fifth best. The rhythm is right, and while cats are notorious leapers, they don't wear capes.

How will we know which books to choose in teaching or modeling voice? That's an important question, for some books are far richer in voice than others, and if what we read does not touch our students, they will be understandably confused about what voice is or why we care about it. So, choose with care. Choose what you love, what you cannot bear to put down, what makes you laugh or cry. Think of the books you give as gifts or those you go back to more than one time. If you do not choose what you love, text in which you can lose yourself, reading will be a chore. You'll feel as if you are standing alone on the stage, reading to a silent auditorium.

When I need a brief mental vacation, I often turn to David Sedaris because his dark, dry humor makes me laugh:

When my family first moved to North Carolina, we lived in a rented house three blocks from the school where I would begin the third grade. My mother made friends with one of the neighbors, but one seemed enough for her. Within a year we would move again and, as she explained, there wasn't much point in getting too close to people we would have to say good-bye to. (2004, 3)

In a more reflective mood, I might turn to Barbara Kingsolver. This passage from her remarkable "Letter to My Mother" lets me see the world through from two perspectives—both achingly familiar:

I am sitting on your lap and you are crying. *Thank you, honey, thank you,* you keep saying, rocking back and forth as you hold me in the kitchen chair. I've brought you flowers: the sweet peas you must have spent all spring trying to grow, training them up the trellis in the yard. You had nothing to work with but abundant gray rains and the patience of a young wife at home with pots and pans and small children, trying to create just one beautiful thing . . . I climbed up the wooden trellis and picked the flowers. Every one. They are gone already, wilting in my hand as you hold me close in the potato-smelling kitchen, and your tears are damp in my hair but you never say a single thing but *Thank you.* (2002, 162)

If we are going to convince our students that voice is not just for personal writing or memoir, we must seek out examples to demonstrate that this is so. Voice in nonfiction writing comes from knowing a topic well and caring about that topic deeply. One writer who more than satisfies those criteria is David Quammen, whose writing is irresistibly entertaining—and often chilling. In *Monster of God*, Quammen argues that we may have only a limited number of years in which to see firsthand the majesty of large predators, such as the lions of Gir, in western India. His data are compelling, but it is the voice that ultimately convinces me, for Quammen has a transcendental understanding of our relationship to the wild—and to wild things:

The road dust, which is fine like ground coriander and inches deep, takes the marks of the lion's big, four-toed paws. Pug marks of such size generally indicate an adult male, so picture him that way: a large tom with a sparse mane. Maybe the mane is blackish, setting off his face against all the brown. Imagine a loose, confident gait. His belly hangs low, his shoulders rise and fall like pistons, each step is placed soundlessly. If a lion strides through the forest and no one is there to see him, is he still kingly? The pug marks say yes. (2003, 20)

As I noted earlier, information-only books, such as encyclopedias, do not need voice to lure us in. Other books live on the edge; their popularity is not assured. Not even something as semitechnical as a handbook or style manual can count on a following because to use such a book regularly you must be teaching or editing, or you must care quite a lot more about usage and punctuation than your average reader probably will (or, like me, you have a quirky sense of what's amusing). Such books rely on voice as a tool to attract readers' attention—and our students need examples to show them how this works.

Bill Walsh's book *The Elephants of Style* is a case in point. Walsh is the copy chief for national news at the *Washington Post* and the author of *Lapsing Into a Comma*. His delivery is more George Burns than Bob Hope, which is to say, you have to figure out for yourself where the jokes are. By his own admission, Walsh is a bit of a stickler when it comes to usage, but he makes good points:

> *He only had three beers* is conversational and understandable, but technically it means *He had three beers and did nothing else*. In writing, *He had only three beers* is more precise. (2004, 200)

Sometimes I find myself saying, "Come on—how important is *that?*" But in the end, Walsh wins me over because he is always (annoyingly enough) right. Sometimes, he's also humorous, as when he reminds us that while many people object to the use of the first-person pronoun *I*, it is infinitely preferable to using "*this writer* or other such silliness." (69) He goes on to say that "one is supposed to avoid referring to one's audience as anything other than *one*." But adds—"*You* know that's ridiculous, right?" Thank you, yes, one *does* know. This writer knows, too.

I like a person who can make issues of usage humorous; I never had a single teacher who did that. It's the humor, the voice, that helps me recall many of Walsh's editorial tips—such as this one: "Starting a sentence with a conjunction is a literary device that can be overused. And it can be annoying. But there's nothing inherently evil about it." (67) And I have the feeling he could go on all day like that. But I wouldn't mind if he did.

When we teach voice by example, we need to use books like *The Elephants of Style*. We need to see—and to show our students—how voice can transform a handbook on grammar and usage into something nearly as readable as a novel. You might not read Walsh's book cover to cover; I'm not sure I would either. But it is a book I reach for frequently, it's one I recommend, it's one I read for fun (even when I'm not dying to know when ending with a preposition is preferable), and I have given it as a gift. That's a high score in voice no matter how you slice it.

At the most fundamental level, when we honor voice, we show profound respect for what students have to say. That's because voice is not really about strategy. Voice is about telling the truth. Truth is not about how much Roy paid for the car or what time Lucille was arrested. Truth is Nikki commenting on her Paraguay project, telling us that if she'd had Brazil, it would have been easy, that life isn't fair, and projects aren't fair—especially this one—and it wouldn't hurt, by God, for someone to keep this in mind next time. "Your own voice," Amy Tan tells us, "is one that seeks a personal truth, one only you can obtain. That truth comes from your own experience, your own observations, and when you find it, if it really is true and specific to you, you may be surprised that others find it to be true as well" (2003, 296). Truth is the soul of voice. And while it is probably among those things that cannot be taught directly, it can be valued. Truth thrives in a classroom atmosphere in which it is safe to share writing, where students know their writing will be received with respect and acceptance.

Where truth thrives, individuality also flourishes. In teaching voice, we need to notice and celebrate differences in students' texts. We need to give student writers freedom to choose their own topics, to develop topics in their own way, and to congratulate them when they do so, even if the outcome is not what we expected. *Especially* when the outcome is not what we expected.

In showing students what we mean by individuality, we need to model and appreciate contrast. This is the main reason for sharing a wide range of voices, not just a bouquet but a vast and expansive garden of voices, each one a little different from the rest. I love it, and want students to love it, that Ernest Hemingway builds meaning through layers of short sentences:

> Then he began to pity the great fish that he had hooked. He is wonderful and strange and who knows how old he is, he thought. Never have I had such a strong fish or one who acted so strangely. Perhaps he is too wise to jump. He could ruin me by jumping or by a wild rush. But perhaps he has been hooked many times before and he knows that this is how he should make his fight. (1952/1980, 48–49)

And Dylan Thomas makes us maneuver through a forest of dependent clauses until we slide, breathless but happy, into a snowy noun-verb ending:

> Years and years and years ago, when I was a boy, when there were wolves in Wales, and birds the colour of red-flannel petticoats whisked past the harp-shaped hills, when we sang and wallowed all night and day in caves that smelt like Sunday afternoons in damp front farmhouse parlours and we chased, with the jawbones of deacons, the English and the bears, before the motor-car, before the wheel, before the duchess-faced horse, when we rode the daft and happy hills bareback, it snowed and it snowed. (1978/1993)

If I teach students to recognize and love differences like these, maybe they will recognize and love what is unique and extraordinary in their own work. And from that self-love comes confidence.

Because every text and every personal writing experience expands our understanding, we teach ourselves about voice forever. Learning about voice is not like learning about participles. We can never master it. Nor can we look it up in the index, check out the reference, and say, "Oh, yes—I remember now." We learn by listening, by writing, and by reading. Reading, just reading for the sheer joy of it, is among the least valued but most worthwhile kinds of professional development.

Only when we teach ourselves to read with a good eye and ear, when we come to see, hear, and feel voice in our very bones, can we begin to offer our students useful feedback. In responding to the method acting piece included earlier, I might say, "Nikki, I love this parody—*To shop or not to shop*—it made me laugh, and I could see that actor's 'placid' face in my mind when you used those words." I don't want to simply say, "Great voice!" because this does not tell Nikki what moved me or why. Writers need to know the precise moment at which we react, and what it is exactly that we feel. Writers are forever asking themselves, "Is anyone there?" We must assure them that unlike the actor playing Hamlet, we are very much at home as we read their work.

We know how important comments are when we write ourselves. Every time I have a piece of writing published, it is thrilling for me until . . . nothing happens. The phone does not ring, no bells sound, no sirens erupt. I wait for someone out there in the big, wide world to say, "Your book! I read your book!" My all-time favorite response came from a colleague, Sally Shorr, a gifted teacher for whose understanding of writing process I have boundless respect. I had sent her a copy of *Creating Writers*, and she emailed back, "I was gardening when the book came. I opened the package and read the first three chapters before I even took my gloves off." I felt like dancing. I wish for every writer a reader like Sally. If every student had such a reader, we would be awash in voice.

Voice is a gift, and must be received as such. When a writer dares to put her heart in her words, we must respond. Garrison Keillor once wrote that "when your true love writes, '*Dear Light of My Life, Joy of My Heart, O Lovely Pulsating Core of my Sensate Life*,' some response is called for" (1989, 138). It takes courage to write with voice, the same sort of courage it takes to declare our love, for we risk being rejected, or worse, ignored. We do not have to embrace everything our students write, but we do have to acknowledge it. "This moment had me laughing hysterically" and "I can sense the relief you felt" are very different but equally useful comments.

What if there *is* no voice? Remember Hansel & Gretel's wicked stepmother in the old fairy tale? When the hungry ragamuffins came home from scrounging in the woods with their baskets empty, no strawberries, she told them they must go back until they found some. Granted, she wasn't much fun, and we don't like her, even a little, but she had a point. We have to keep looking, too. And when we teach ourselves to look, it is surprising how much we begin to see. For the wise teacher, the tiniest beginning is a place from which to build. The wise teacher knows that even when there is not voice within the text, there is voice within the writer.

Such faith is highly apparent in Lucy Calkins' text *The Conferring Handbook*. In a remarkable scaffolding conference, teacher Zoe White questions, coaxes, reinforces, summarizes, and nudges primary writer Bryanna from a picture of a huge flower beside a tiny apartment building to a full-blown, multiple-detailed story of coming home with her mother, going up the steps, seeing the doorman, and getting a Tootsie Roll Pop—with illustrations to match (2003, 2).

Zoe has many choices when she first looks at the little sketch Bryanna has done. She could comment on what she sees—a big flower overshadowing the tiny building ("Wow—what a big flower!")—and let it go. She could say something pleasantly encouraging though not particularly helpful to Bryanna, like "Good job coloring your flower!" She could note what is missing, thereby conveying her disappointment: "I hope you are going to write something to go with your picture!" She does none of these things.

Instead, step by step, she helps Bryanna to think of herself as a writer: "Well, Bryanna, you are so smart to be making a story here on the paper that is about something in your own life." (3) And later, after the writer has shared some of her story orally: "Oh, my goodness, Bryanna. Do you realize what a story you have here? At first, I just thought you went into your building and that was that. But there is so much more!"

Zoe gets excited, not just about what Bryanna has drawn so far, but about the writing that is literally blossoming in this young writer's mind, and she helps Bryanna to see all that her writing can become. Her enthusiasm and her trust are wonderfully contagious. We can get excited too, and help our writers to hear the voice that is just a whisper now, but that can become a song. We can find the berries if we look hard enough, and we must not give up until we do. After all, there is a lot at stake: everything.

In *Shades of Black: A Celebration of Our Children* (2000), author Sandra L. Pinkney shows us that black is not one color, but a multitude. It might be the "velvety orange in a peach" or the "coppery brown in a pretzel" or the "radiant brassy yellow in popcorn." Voice is like that. It comes in many colors, boasting differences both spectacular and subtle. It is our history, our culture, our family, our spirit, our deepest self. It is all that we are, and the promise of all that we can become. When we honor our children's voices, we honor the beauty of that diversity.

Speaking As Renee

BARRY LANE

I have a confession to make. Twenty-five years ago, I was a woman. No, I didn't dress like a woman and I didn't talk like a woman. I wrote like a woman.

A local women's newspaper had a weekly column called "First Person," which encouraged readers to write in and tell their stories. Just as a joke, I submitted a piece called "The Orgasm Index," under the name of Renee Newmarch. In the piece, I discussed a recent news report that quoted a study saying married women had more orgasms than single women. I wrote that I had discussed this report with my husband and we had a silly tiff about it; then my Renee imagined news commentator Peter Jennings saying, "The Orgasm Index is down five points today due to moderate to heavy husband swapping."

Despite the attention it received, I didn't think it was a very good piece of writing. It certainly didn't have much of a point. But it did have that elusive quality that makes people want to read something. It had voice.

A week later, there was a gift certificate in the mail and a letter of congratulations. My career as a woman writer had begun.

In the weeks that followed, I published at least a dozen articles under the name Renee Newmarch. I explored my first attempts at motherhood, a mouse problem, my harrowing experiences hitchhiking, and even my startling discovery that my great-grandmother had been a prostitute in Victorian England. No subject was too monumental or too trivial for Renee's pen. She spun philosophical discussions from doing laundry and wove global issues into a daily trip to the supermarket. No matter how confusing or mean or crazy life got, she found time to tell the world about it.

I loved writing in Renee's voice. It awoke in me a passion for the life I wanted to be living. I was a twenty-seven-year-old single, lonely man living in a seven by forty-two-foot trailer, and Renee was a daredevil young mother in her early thirties, who had just bought her first house and had just had her first child. I hid from life; Renee embraced it.

The masquerade ended one day with a letter from the editor-in-chief of the magazine. She loved my writing (Renee's writing) and wanted me to meet with her to discuss writing larger pieces. I toyed with the idea of dressing as a woman or sending a woman friend as a stand-in, but both ideas seemed equally immoral and ludicrous, and I quickly abandoned them.

I decided to try a radical new approach. I stopped writing in Renee's voice and wrote three pieces in my own voice. After all, the paper had published many columns by men. I had a lot to say about the world, and I had "real" experiences to write about, unlike some other columnists I knew. All three pieces were rejected.

I looked at the growing pile of polite rejection letters and decided I needed the truth, so I called the newspaper and asked for the editor.

"You're a good writer," she said. "You're clever, but the pieces aren't quite the right tone for the paper."

"What tone are you looking for?" I asked.

"Funny," she replied.

"OK," I said. "I can try funny." I didn't let on that I had already tried funny in the last three pieces. "By the way," I added casually, "I'm friends with Renee Newmarch."

"YOU KNOW RENEE NEWMARCH?" The woman could barely contain her enthusiasm. "WHERE IS SHE?"

"I don't quite know. Last I heard she went to Egypt. I'll let her know you asked about her when she gets back."

"Please, please do. We love her writing. Tell her to call me anytime."

As I hung up the phone, I felt a pang of jealousy for Renee Newmarch, the woman I had created. I also came to the sad realization that I could write with more honesty, more humor, and more sense of reality in the voice of a fictitious woman than in my own male voice. What did this say about my sad, pathetic, lonely existence?

A year later I was married. A month after that, I left my trailer, moved to Vermont, bought a house, and started raising my own family. In short, I started living the life Renee Newmarch had only written about. Looking back, I now realize my playful columns were a type of written rehearsal for this richer life I had finally begun living. And though I never wrote in Renee's voice again, in my heart I know she is still living with me.

Putting on a mask frees a writer from the fetters of his own existence and can lead to deeper understandings, self-realizations, and what-ifs. Though I would not encourage students to deceive editors or readers as I did, I would coax them to explore voices beyond their own. This playful masquerading can eventually help them to hear the one true voice that lies waiting to be discovered inside them.

BARRY LANE *has taught students at nearly every grade level (including adult writers), and is known internationally for his humorous, inventive, and engaging workshops on voice and the art of revision. He is the author of numerous books loved by teachers and students alike, includ-ing* The Reviser's Toolbox, after THE END, 51 Wacky We-Search Reports, The Tor-toise and the Hare Continued, *and* Why We Must Run with Scissors. *Barry is the founder and president of Discover Writing, a publishing house that also provides writing work-shops throughout the country.*

Abeel, Samantha. 2003. *My Thirteenth Winter: A Memoir.* New York: Orchard Books.

Ackerman, Diane. 2001. *Cultivating Delight: A Natural History of My Garden.* New York: HarperCollins.

———. 2004. *An Alchemy of Mind.* New York: Scribner.

Ballenger, Bruce. 2004. *The Curious Researcher,* 4th ed. New York: Pearson.

Barry, Lynda. 1998. *The Good Times Are Killing Me.* Seattle: Sasquatch Books.

Boyle, David, & Anita Roddick. 2004. *Numbers.* West Sussex, UK: Anita Roddick Books.

Brallier, Jess, and Sally Chabert. 1996. *Presidential Wit and Wisdom.* New York: Penguin Books.

Brodie, Deborah, ed. 1997. *Writing Changes Everything.* New York: St. Martin's Press.

Calkins, Lucy, Amanda Hartman, Zoë White, and the Units of Study Co-Authors. 2003. *The Conferring Handbook.* Portsmouth, NH: firsthand.

Cisneros, Sandra. 1989. *The House on Mango Street.* New York: Vintage Books.

Clark, Hiro, ed. 1993. *Picasso in His Words.* San Francisco: HarperCollins.

Elbow, Peter. 1986. *Embracing Contraries.* New York: Oxford University Press.

Facklam, Margery. 2001. *Spiders and Their Websites.* Boston: Little, Brown.

Fox, Mem. 1993. *Radical Reflections.* Orlando, FL: Harcourt Brace.

Fraser, Jane, and Donna Skolnick. 1994. *On Their Way: Celebrating Second Graders as They Read and Write.* Portsmouth, NH: Heinemann.

Goldberg, Natalie. 1990. *Wild Mind: Living the Writer's Life.* New York: Bantam Books.

Graves, Donald H. 1994. *A Fresh Look at Writing.* Portsmouth, NH: Heinemann.

———. 2002. *Testing Is Not Teaching.* Portsmouth, NH: Heinemann.

Haas, Jessie. 2004. *Hoofprints: Horse Poems.* New York: HarperCollins.

Hemingway, Ernest. 1952/1980. *The Old Man and the Sea*. New York: Simon & Schuster.

Hesse, Karen. 1999. *"Come on, rain!"* New York: Scholastic.

Hewlitt Packard. 2002. *The Laser Printer Customer Handbook*. Palo Alto, CA: Hewlitt Packard Corporation.

Hillenbrand, Laura. 2001. *Seabiscuit*. New York: Ballantine Books.

Hillocks, George Jr. 2002. *The Testing Trap: How State Writing Assessments Control Learning*. New York: Teachers College.

Keillor, Garrison. 1987. *Leaving Home: A Collection of Lake Wobegon Stories*. New York: Viking Penguin.

———. 1989. *We Are Still Married: Stories & Letters*. New York: Viking.

King, Stephen. 2000. *On Writing: A Memoir of the Craft*. New York: Scribner.

Kingsolver, Barbara. 2002. *Small Wonder*. New York: HarperCollins.

Kuralt, Charles. 1995. *Charles Kuralt's America*. New York: G. P. Putnam's Sons.

Lamott, Anne. 1995. *Bird by Bird: Some Instructions on Writing and Life*. New York: Doubleday.

Lobel, Arnold. 1970. *The Frog and Toad Treasury*. New York: Barnes & Noble Books.

Mead-Ferro, Muffy. 2004. *Confessions of a Slacker Mom*. Cambridge, MA: Da Capo Lifelong Books.

Moore, Kathleen Dean. 1995. *Riverwalking: Reflections on Moving Water*. New York: Harcourt Brace.

Murray, Donald M. 1982. "Grant Your Students Their Writing Rights." Pgs. 175–176 in *Learning by Teaching*. Portsmouth, NH: Boynton/Cook Publishers.

———. 2004. *A Writer Teaches Writing*, Revised 2d ed. Boston: Heinle.

Musgrave, Susan, ed. 2001. *Nerves Out Loud: Critical Moments in the Lives of Seven Teen Girls*. New York: Annick Press.

National Writing Project and Carl Nagin. 2003. *Because Writing Matters: Improving Student Writing in Our Schools*. San Francisco: John Wiley & Sons, Inc.

Paulsen, Gary. 1994. *Winterdance: The Fine Madness of Running the Iditarod*. Orlando, FL: Harcourt Brace.

———, ed. 2003. *Shelf Life: Stories by the Book*. New York: Simon & Schuster Books for Young Readers.

Peck, Richard. 2002. *Invitations to the World: Teaching and Writing for the Young*. New York: Dial Books.

Pinkney, Sandra L. 2000. *Shades of Black: A Celebration of Our Children*. New York: Scholastic.

Proulx, Annie. 2002. *That Old Ace in the Hole*. New York: Scribner.

Pukite, John. 2002. *A Field Guide to Pigs*. New York: Penguin Books.

Quammen, David. 2001. *The Boilerplate Rhino*. New York: Simon and Schuster.

———. 2003. *Monster of God: The Man-Eating Predator in the Jungles of History and the Mind*. New York: W. W. Norton.

Ray, Katie Wood. 2002. *What You Know by Heart: How to Develop Curriculum for Your Writing Workshop*. Portsmouth, NH: Heinemann.

Rooney, Andy. 2000. *My War*. New York: Public Affairs.

Routman, Regie. 2000. *Conversations: Strategies for Teaching, Learning, and Evaluating*. Portsmouth, NH: Heinemann.

Sagan, Carl. 1980. *Cosmos*. New York: Random House.

Sedaris, David. 2004. *Dress Your Family in Corduroy and Denim*. New York: Little, Brown.

Seinfeld, Jerry. 1993. *SeinLanguage*. New York: Bantam Books.

Shorr, Sally. September 15, 2004. Personal communication.

Spandel, Vicki. 2005. *Creating Writers*, 4th ed. Boston: Allyn and Bacon.

Strunk, William, and E. B. White. 1979. *The Elements of Style*, 3d ed. New York: Macmillan.

Tan, Amy. 2003. *The Opposite of Fate: Memories of a Writing Life*. New York: G. P. Putnam's Sons.

"Ten Questions for Laura Hillenbrand." September 3, 2003. *The New York Times*.

Thomas, Dylan. 1978–1993. *A Child's Christmas in Wales*. London: Orion Children's Books.

Thomas, Lewis. 1995. *The Medusa and the Snail*. New York: Penguin Books.

Walsh, Bill. 2004. *The Elephants of Style: A Trunkload of Tips on the Big Issues and Gray Areas of Contemporary American English*. New York: McGraw-Hill.

Wiley, Mark. 2000. "The Popularity of Formulaic Writing (and Why We Need to Resist)." *English Journal* (September).

Wysocki, Charles. 1994. *Heartland*. New York: Artisan.

Yagoda, Ben. 2004. *The Sound on the Page: Style and Voice in Writing*. New York: HarperCollins.

Brooks, Carellin, 134–35
Bryson, Bill, 84
Burke, Jim, xiii, 91–92
Burns, George, 139
Busy-ness, 10

C
Cain, James M., 134
Calkins, Lucy, 142
Campbell, Bebe Moore, 137
Carson, Rachel, 13
Catcher in the Rye, 27
Censorship, 27–28
Charles Kuralt's America, 16–17
Checklists, in assessment, 47, 100–4
Chicago Manual of Style, The, 46–47
Child's Christmas in Wales, A, 6–7
Ciardi, John, 110
Cisneros, Sandra, 81, 89, 134, 136
Clarity, rubrics and, 101
Classroom layout, nourishing writing
    through, 42
Clever Hans, 111
Collaboraphobia, 99
Collaboration, writing process and, 99
Collard, Sneed B., xiii, 89
    rewriting process used by, 83
    writing as a dance, 118
    writing process used by, 60–62
Collins, Billy, 137
Come On, Rain!, 135–36
Como, Perry, 23
Compassion
    in commentary, 106
    quality assessment and, 94, 95–96
Concentration, 83
Conditions that nourish writing,
    establishing, 41–43
Conferring Handbook, The, 142
Confessions of a Slacker Mom, 25
Confidence, writers and, 44–45, 72
Conner, Flannery, 135
Consistency, 48
Continuity, writing and, 79
Conversation
    craving of, 21–22
    nourishing writing through, 42
Conversations, 14, 82

Cooking, by inspiration, 114–15
Cooper, Charles, 123
Corporate writing, 16
Cosby Show, The, 38
Creating Writers, 65, 141
Creativity, 33
"Creepy Spider," 132
Cultivating Delight, 1
Curiosity, 60
Curious Researcher, The, xiii
Curriculum, interrupted writing, 79

D
Daily writing, 45, 46, 71
Darwin, Charles, 5
Daydreaming, 10–11
Dead River (Minnesota), 2
"December: New York City," 17
Deep-Sea Floor, The, 61
Details
    as affecting voice, 134–35
    thinking about terms like, 122
Dialogue, value of authentic, 136
Dolphins, discussion of essay on,
    118–19
Down draft, 92
Drafting, 44, 61
    behaviors, 49
    consistency with, 48
    final drafts, 68
    modeling, 83
    writing process and, 43
Dylan, Bob, 15

E
Ears, reading with, 106
Editing, 48, 61–62
    writing process and, 43
Einstein, Albert, 5
Elbow, Peter, 107
Elements of Style, The, 129, 139
Environment
    creating comfortable space to write
        in, 83–84
    importance of supportive writing,
        41–43
Evaluation. *See* Assessment
Examples of writing, sharing, 19–21

Native Son, 38
Nephila, 17–18
Nerves Out Loud, 134
Newbery Medal, 57
Newkirk, Tom, xiii, 27–28
Newman, Randy, 84
Newmarch, Renee, 143, 144
New York Times, 57
1984, 121
Noise, reverence for, 43–44
Nonfiction writing, voice in, 128,
    138–39
"No Training Wheels," 126–27
Numbers, 93
Numbers obsession, 111
NYPD Blue, 87

O
Objectivity, 132
Observation
    of conditions that nourish writing,
        41–42
    right to *see* others write, 78–92
    topic ideas and, 22–24
    of writing process, importance of,
        42–43
Odell, Lee, 123
"Ode to Horses," 108–9
Off topic, the right to go, 29–39
Oh, Hemingway!, 37–38
Oral reading, revealing selves through,
    47–48
Oregon State Writing Assessment, 73
"Orgasm Index, The," 143
Originality, voice and, 33
Orlean, Susan, 110, 131
Ornstein, Bob, xiii, 37–39
Orwell, George, 57

P
Passion
    in commentary, 106
    lack of, in formula writing, 120
    reading with, value of, 136–37
    value of writing with, 82–83
Paulsen, Gary, 78, 81, 89
    believes that books saved his life, 6
    and the Iditarod, 7–8, 24–25

Peck, Richard, 22, 86, 90
Perception, quality assessment and, 94
Perfectionism, 41
Personality, voice as being like, 133
Personalizing
    topics, 32–33
    topics, difficulty with, 80
    writing process, right to personalize,
        40–62
Personal narratives, 48
Perspective
    voice and, 33
    voice coming from, 132
Picasso, Pablo, 88, 90
Pigs, discussion of essay on, 116–18
Pinkney, Sandra L., 142
Platypus, Probably, A, 61
Pliny the Elder, 70–71
Poking around, 22
Popularity of Formulaic Writing, The, 114
Porter, Cole, 84
Portfolios, 41–42
    managing writing with, 46
    in quality assessment, 97–98
    sample writing, 130
Power, voice as, 133
Powerful writing, assessment and, 102
Prairie Builders, The, 61
Predictability in formulaic writing,
    115
Prewriting, 44
    behaviors, 49
    consistency with, 48
    writing process and, 43
Problem solving, writing as, 85
Professional development, assessment
    as, 98–99
Prompts
    assessment and nobility of, 29–31
    lack of voice and, 31
Proulx, Annie, 86, 90
Provocative writing, assessment and,
    102
Publishing, 48
Publishing guidelines, importance of,
    46
Pukite, John, 116–18
Purpose, writing and, 19–20

Vonnegut, Kurt, 127

W
Wagner, Richard, 17
Walsh, Bill, 139
War Admiral, 7
Washington Post, 139
Webs, writing process as, 65, 68
What You Know By Heart, 78
White, E. B., 129
White, Zoe, 142
"Who Swims with the Tuna," discussion of, 118–19
"Why Pigs?", discussion of, 116
Wiggins, Grant, 102
Wiley, Mark, 114
Willamette Week, 16, 35
Wilson, David, 84
Woods, Rachel Jordan, 107
Woolf, George, 7
Wright, Richard, 38
Writer, focusing on the, 124
Writers
    assessors as, 105–6
    being gentle with themselves, 87
    confidence and, 44–45, 72
    fourth grade writers, advice from, 57–58
    high school writers, advice from, 58–59
    journals, writers as keepers of, 23
    professional writers do, examining what, 122–23
    writing what you know, value of, 82
Writer's block, 12–13
Writer's groups, 61–62
Write Source 2000, 46
Writing. *See also* Writing process
    an event in some classrooms, 71
    conditions for, 41–43
    confidence and, 44–45

    daily, 45, 46, 71
    emphasis on, varied, 79
    goals of, xii
    habits of starting, 10–11
    hardest things about, 18–19
    as hard work, 91–92
    journey, thinking of writing as a, 122
    philosophy for, 114
    as problem solving, 85
    sample student reflections, 50, 51–56
    teaching, reasons for, xi–xii
    value of, xi–xii
Writing across the curriculum, 71
Writing Changes Everything, 29, 63
Writing folders, 46, 72
Writing from the heart, 131
Writing instruction, relationship between assessment and, 126–27
Writing process
    assessment and, 98–99, 126–27
    environment, importance of supportive, 41–43
    freedom and, 57
    individualizing, 50
    right to personalize, 40–62
    step-by-step approaches and, 48–49
    steps, 43, 49–51
    student reflections, sample, 50, 51–56
    as web, 65, 68
    a writer talks about his process, 60–62
Writing workshop, structure and, 45–46
Wysocki, Charles, xi, 10, 125

Y
Yagoda, Ben, 106